In My Mother's Shoes

Alison Walsh is a native of Dublin, where
she lives with her husband and three children.
She has been an editor for many years and is a regular
contributor to the *Sunday Independent* books page.
In My Mother's Shoes is her first book.

Alison Walsh

In My Mother's Shoes

PAN BOOKS

First published 2010 by Macmillan

This edition published 2011 by Pan Books
an imprint of Pan Macmillan, a division of Pan Macmillan Limited
Pan Macmillan, 20 New Wharf Road, London N1 9RR
Basingstoke and Oxford
Associated companies throughout the world
www.panmacmillan.com

ISBN 978-0-330-50942-8

3 5 7 9 8 6 4 2

A CIP catalogue record for this book is available from
the British Library.

Typeset by SetSystems Limited, Saffron Walden, Essex
Printed in the UK by CPI Mackays, Chatham ME5 8TD

To the two strong women in my life,

Anne and Pauline,

with love

Contents

Introduction

'Our members display a wonderful variety of talent and activities, these range from arts and crafts to matters domestic, from doings on the farm or in the garden to those of public concern. Adult education and debates, travel talks and Good Works performed in aid of charities – all these mingle with the lighter side of Guild programmes, which show that members often enjoy the relaxation of a party, dance or outing. Many, too, are keen on music, play-acting and miming.'

Irish Countrywomens Association
Secretary's Report, 1954

When I tell people that I'm writing a book about motherhood their eyes glaze over and you sense them wondering
why I'm not writing about hang-gliding off the top of
Everest or going to live with the Kulo-Kulo tribe of the
western Amazon. My brother-in-law thinks that I'm
secretly writing an erotic thriller, possibly unable to
believe that anyone could devote an entire book to this
most mundane of subjects. After all, mothering is something that vast numbers of us do, quietly absorbed in the
humdrum world of washing, cleaning, cooking, childrearing, buggy pushing, going down the shops in the kind
of ageless domestic ritual that feminism and all of modern
life has not succeeded in budging. Once we become
mothers, whether we work or not, we find ourselves
inexorably pulled back into the world of the washing
machine and Hoover. I am unlikely, for the next ten
years, to win the Vendée Globe yacht race, or to devote
myself to the starving of Calcutta; I spend most of my
time in the post office, or the supermarket, buying shoes,
finding pencils, helping with homework. What could be

more boring as a subject? And yet motherhood is an unsung and unnoticed job which is heroic in its displays of management, compassion, psychological insight, love and support; and, yes, often the locus of other, darker emotions, rage, depression, envy, low self-esteem. Motherhood is often dismissed as being not worthy of consideration as it is simply not goal-oriented enough: there are no quarterly figures to be pored over, no yearly sales targets, no productivity goals. The achievements of motherhood aren't measurable – so many well-adjusted children were produced between 2005 and 2010, with a year-on-year gain in good manners and with several more thousands going forward – and yet people's lives and happiness quite literally depend on their mothers. The shelves groan under the weight of books by those who endured terrible things at the hands of their mothers, and others credit their success and happiness to that most central figure in their lives.

Which is why the book I originally set out to write is not the book that I ended up with, to my surprise and occasional discomfort. When I started, I thought I would impart my considerable wisdom about motherhood, gleaned from raising my own three children, in a lighthearted, breezy fashion, as befitted my status as a happy mother who was enjoying focusing on home and family after years at the office coalface.

But then I realized that there was something wrong with this picture: playing motherhood for laughs didn't quite cut it when, in fact, I had found so much of it hard going, struggling to reconcile my rosy expectations with the rather less romantic reality and with the crushing realization that I was a less-than-perfect mother. Thus, whilst hopefully not full of Dostoevskian gloom, this book will end up being a more realistic, less frighteningly jolly picture of what motherhood is really like, of the unvarnished truth behind the cheery talk over coffee and scones in the local café.

We tell ourselves a lot of lies as mothers – that childbirth isn't painful and messy and traumatic; that we bond with our babies instantly because we are 'natural' mothers; that we adore every burp and fart, marvel at every milestone and happily play Sticklebricks and Lego with them for hours without nearly passing out with boredom; that we never fight with them, or behave like Godzilla because they haven't tidied up their bedroom; we lie to ourselves that because we love our children, we also love motherhood – all of the time.

I should know: I have spent quite a lot of time lying to myself, telling myself that this life, which I have chosen after all, is just perfect! Hating myself for resenting the narrowness of my horizons as a stay-at-home mother and sometimes freelance editor and writer; loving my children but chafing against their never-ending need for me; comparing myself to other, patient, gentle mothers and wishing I was like them. I wonder whether I will ever be 'myself' again, a person separate from my duties and responsibilities to my children, from my desire to give them everything I can, whilst secretly wondering if it'll ever end.

Over the last five years, since I left the office, clutching my department store voucher and bouquet of flowers, I have had ample time to ponder, in snatched moments, why I've chosen this life. And why, in the twenty-first century, I am doing more or less the same things as my mother and grandmother did before me. As I learn more about myself as a mother, I've begun to want to understand them better, now that I am in their shoes. I know what it is like to be bored, lonely and stressed, as I know my mother felt, to feel that I can't face making another dinner, to feel guilt at my impatience with my youngest son, and shame at how often I match his screams with my own when he stamps his foot, or at my choosing to zone out my eldest's ceaseless chatter as I pretend to listen to his explanations of the lesser-known rules of PlayStation, in defiance of the childcare manuals, which tell me that I should 'actively listen' to my child. I know what it is like to love my children more than I would have thought possible, and yet to be unsure if my children know it, if I'm telling them just how great I think they are, not that they've left their smelly socks under the bed again. I want to be a better mother and yet, like my mother and grandmother, I'm not, I'm just a mother, with flaws aplenty.

And this is why this book has ended up being not just

about me, but about three mothers: my grandmother, my mother and me. As I hover over the freezer in Tesco, wondering whether it will be peas or sweetcorn, I remember standing behind my mother in the queue in Grehan's butchers in Blackrock, the little seaside town in which I grew up. I would examine the diagram of the parts of the cow on the wall as my mother ordered mince and stewing steak and other thrifty cuts of meat, before going to pay the man who sat in a glass-walled booth at the front of the shop with a till that made a loud 'ping' when he opened it. We would then cross the road, my mother extending her hand automatically to take mine, to the tiny shop on the main street, in whose window was displayed a solitary cake stand bearing a handful of brown scones. From behind the high wooden counter of this nondescript little shop, an elderly lady would produce a stream of home-baked bread, and my mother would select a couple of loaves and maybe a handful of the scones, nothing exotic, mind.

As I stand outside the school in a huddle with other mothers, waiting for our children, chatting idly about tennis lessons and homework, I remember my mother doing the same thing: dropping me to school in her battered grey Morris Minor, my little sister smiling and waving goodbye to me out of the window. And, although I know slightly less about Nana, I'm sure she did the same thing, on a bicycle, my mother's hair tied in one of the ridiculously large bows her mother favoured.

As I thought about them both more, I became curious as to what being a mother would have been like for Nana, seventy years ago, the wife of a civil servant in a little country town; or my mother, in a pleasant Dublin suburb; what would we have shared, and what would have divided us? The time frame is sufficiently different to make Ireland another world: Catholic, homely, repressed, quiet, warmly friendly, and now, secular, shiny, acquisitive, brash. My grandmother was born and raised around the corner from where I now live, which seemed to complete the connection between us. However, whereas my neighbourhood encompasses a mix of respectable professionals, little old ladies and gay couples, with the only blot on the landscape being our local friendly drug dealer, her Harold's Cross was a grimy impoverished enclave which, my mother confidently tells me, 'stank', and was thick with coal smoke, and she lived in the bijou two-up-two-downs that are now occupied by architects and solicitors, with her seven siblings.

Nana's early years as a mother were spent in the shadow of the Second World War, or The Emergency as we called it here, a fairly typical Irish euphemism. War didn't mean death or hardship in Ireland in nearly the same way as in the UK, but basically a lack of certain necessities, like fuel, which meant that Nana cooked on a Primus stove, and Granddad Jack booked a taxi to visit clients, which only had enough petrol to take him to the picturesquely named Shillelagh, about ten miles away. Hardly deprivation on the scale endured by others, but there was a certain grey, dormant quality to my mother's world; no heating, hot water, coffee, bananas or oranges, no trips in the car, no nice clothes, the only excitement provided by the occasional huge unexploded mine which would roll up onto the beach, out of the Irish Sea.

In her turn, my mother was a mother in a middle-class Dublin suburb during the 1970s, having been forced out of her state job on marriage. She hadn't gone to university as her father told her she wouldn't need to; since she would only be getting married, it would all be a bit of a waste. Thus, after a glimpse of life's possibilities provided by her work at the national airline, she, like all of her friends, embraced her destiny and became a housewife, because that's what you did then. In her pleasant suburb by the sea there were coffee mornings, crab salads, choux pastry rings, sweet German wines like Black Tower, which were considered the height of sophistication then, culottes and maxi dresses. There were diamond-patterned sweaters, golf clubs, drinks with the neighbours, families who were peculiar, plenty who had religious fetishes, or who stayed up all night watching *Man About the House*, all accompanied by the constant drone of the lawn mower.

And me, I have it all: all the opportunities my mother and grandmother never had, a comfortable middle-class upbringing, a university education and a profession, and yet, like my mother and grandmother, I orbit daily between school and shop; this age-old connection persists, even though times have changed.

But I have another reason for wanting to write about Nana and Mum, one that goes to the heart of being a mother. As I learn more about myself as a mother, I have reached back into my own childhood and remembered my relationship with my mother and her relationship with her mother. I wonder which of their dramas will play out in my own life and in my relationship with my only daughter. I have become interested in how the mother I am today is a result of the mother my grandmother was, and my own mother, and in how much and how little has changed.

When I was a child, Nana was a real constant in my life. She was a steadying presence, my mother having been derailed by my brother's autism and unable to focus on much else other than trying to keep some of his behavioural tics in check and catering to his bizarre culinary needs. Nana would take me for regular Saturday-morning trips to Bewley's café on Grafton Street, for my favourite meringues, to be served by a colossal Dublin woman with a tiny frilled waitresses' cap perched incongruously on her head, size nines flapping along the ground as she tottered along, pushing a cake trolley towards us like an outsize Mrs Overall, with a coffee cream slice on it for Nana and my meringue, a mountain of sugary egg white and cream, with a couple of half grapes in it for health's sake.

Taking my brother and me under her wing, Nana spent a lot of time with both of us, attempting to prevent Ian knocking her head off with a nine-iron when she taught us golf, or constructing a swimming pool for us in their country home out of a galvanized steel cattle tank. When we visited her in Waterford, the town to which she'd moved with Granddad because of his job, we would lie underneath her classic dusky-pink eiderdown, as she tested my spelling and filled our heads with a stream of all kinds of nonsense about how President Kennedy was a personal friend of hers, simply because her brother's wife's sister-in-law's second cousin had once shaken his hand on his visit to Ireland. As a teenager, when she had moved to Dublin to be closer to us, I would mope over to her house in a nearby suburb and moan a bit, whereupon she would announce that she had just the cure, producing a large bottle of Powers Gold Label Whiskey from the sideboard, taking a cursory glance at the clock before announcing, 'Ah, sure half-eleven's nearly lunchtime,' and pouring a large amount into a tumbler.

For me, Nana wasn't a constant embarrassment, or a smothering, over-attentive mother, she was a source of amusement, comfort and mild irritation. She was Nana.

And yet to my mother, her bookish, reserved only daughter, Nana's larger-than-life persona was a source of mortification and dread in equal measure. She spent her entire life in the shadow of the Queen of Showbiz, enduring her peacock-like showing off, Tourette's-like inability to stay quiet and gift for the gently inappropriate remark. My mother stubbornly resisted Nana's constant attempts to ringlet her hair, to plonk some ridiculously oversized bow on top, and dress her in frothy outfits; she banged deadly on the piano keys when Nana tried to pass on her love of music, refusing to 'join in' the purgatory of the musical evenings and sing-songs which Nana so loved.

As adults, their relationship was fraught, tense, full of irritated comments on my mother's side, and enraged silences at yet another of Nana's unsuitable remarks – utter nonsense like being sure the Pope had a secret family stashed in the Vatican, or that the IRA had taken over the local supermarket, which the rest of us would let gently drift over our heads, but which Mum seemed unable to let go of, like an angry terrier with a bone. And yet, as Nana's only child, my mother was bound to her, all the time chafing at the proximity; but when it came to it and Nana was too old to cope alone, my mother had a granny flat built on the side of our house, where Nana lived for the last ten years of her life, listening to Mass in the local parish church, handily transmitted over a short-wave radio; making appalling dinners for herself, which should have hastened her demise, but which seemed to extend it, her insides coated with salty bacon and overcooked cabbage; and doing little jobs in her small garden, which she decorated with hubcaps, to nobody's surprise.

Nana was completely baffled as to why she was so irritating to her only daughter and would continue to chirrup away, asking my mother if she thought the cake she'd made might improve a bit with a drop of sherry added, carefully ignoring her daughter's hissed response. So they went on, bound together by duty and responsibility and love, in a peculiar way, like Joan Crawford and Bette Davis in *Whatever Happened to Baby Jane*, until Nana's death, aged 91.

*

As the self-righteous daughter, I had wondered why on earth my mother sought to be close to someone whom she could hardly bear the sight of – but now, as a mother myself, I understand. Mum was Nana's daughter, and Nana was her mother, and so she did what was needed. I wonder if my daughter will do the same: will she be willing to push me, aged eighty, along in my bath chair, listening to me witter on about *Gardeners' World*, or will she loathe me beyond measure and cheerfully shove me in the nearest rest home?

I know, deep down, that I have carried on the tradition of strong, eccentric women on my mother's side of the family, from Granny MacNeill, unsmiling in her gabardine coat, frizzy hair and glasses, who had a nervous breakdown every time Nana looked like marrying and leaving her, to Nana's show-must-go-on, sing-your-heart-out personality, to my mother, who has fashioned herself in opposition to her mother, hidden her own strength of character behind a quiet privacy, restraint and love of gardening, whose relationship with her daughter has been forged in spite of the difficulties with her son. I sometimes fear that I will loom large in my daughter's life, like a pantomime dame, with a loud voice and louder clothes, embarrassing her at every turn. Even now I catch myself wanting to comment on the hideous puce tracksuit bottoms she favours instead of the cute jeans, but bite my tongue, avoiding the innate maternal desire to criticize – 'Are you wearing *that*?'

*

However, in spite of the fraught difficulties of their relationships and the hardships of their lives, I want to connect with Nana and Mum in a positive way and not to see them as victims of their circumstances, which is certainly not how they saw themselves. I don't want this book to be a grim trawl through the privations of the 1940s and 1960s, the narrow horizons of holy Catholic Ireland. I also don't want it to be a nostalgic yarn about yesteryear, about how much happier we were with no shoes on our feet, existing on a diet of cabbage and bacon, or how a swift clip on the ear did nobody any harm and how children were much happier when they were third-class citizens. My mother and grandmother were busy, hardworking women, making the most of what life offered and enjoying the company and the support of other women in the same situation.

In delving into the past, a picture emerged for me of Irish women who fought hard to carve out the rights that I now take entirely for granted, who uncomplainingly brought up their large families and formed the centre of their communities in newly independent Ireland. For me, groups of women like the Irish Countrywomens Association, or ICA, epitomize the space between me and Nana and our lives then and now. Nana found her true vocation when she joined the ICA. A formidable organization during the years between the 1940s and the 1970s, it had originally been set up to allow country women a break from their hardworking lives, and to develop skills that might earn them a valuable income to supplement the farm's. Later, it broadened its scope to include city 'guilds' or groupings and became quite a powerful NGO and a rather conservative voice in Irish life. Nana joined in Sligo in the 1950s, as a way of meeting people in the latest new place to which her husband's roving civil service job had brought her.

Country skills were very much the thing in the ICA, and members got involved in rush-weaving, rug-making, jam-making and, for some reason, skin-curing, and thus various members of my family disported items with Fresian patterns on them: my mother had a Fresian handbag and Nana a purse, and my brother was very fond of Foxy, his pet fox, which we later learned was roadkill, which Nana had scraped off the tarmac, stuffed, and presented to her first grandchild as a Christmas present.

When I was a child visiting Nana in Waterford, I was fascinated by her network of ICA friends and their busy and productive lives. The ICA seemed to be a hive of constant, energizing activity. Like elderly air hostesses, they would buzz around the world, attending conferences with countrywomen's groups in other countries, such as Kenya, Estonia or America, from which Nana would return with entertaining stories of bad behaviour and with the contents of the airplane in her Fresian handbag: cutlery, napkins, sugar sachets, tiny cartons of milk, with which she would thriftily fill her fridge and kitchen drawers.

Re-entering the woman's world of the past seemed to be a positive, life-enhancing way to reconnect with Nana and her life, and I did it by consulting the archives of the ICA, stored in our national library. In spite of only being allowed to examine one file at a time by the librarian, who seemed to be convinced that Philbyesque secrets lurked within, I was charmed by the picture that emerged of this community, and the warmth and support it offered to Nana when other avenues were closed to her. I have a job and a profession and yet I have no such community. And I couldn't skin a badger. I have no connection to nature and to rural life – the fauna of my neighbourhood are strictly of the tracksuit variety. I can't bottle veg or preserve strawberries in a million different ways to take me through the winter. I don't set up plays with my friends on ancient Celtic themes, or join in competitions to design the nicest egg cosy. I can't weave a St Brigid's cross out of rushes, or crochet a set of tablemats. I am everything that Nana wasn't – and yet our lives connect in so many ways.

In this book I hope to do her and my mother justice, to look at them as mothers and the job they did, without unleashing my inner adolescent and banging on about all the bad things they did to me. I want to use them as a touchstone to write about my own experiences. Above all, I want to write as honestly as I can about the real work of motherhood.

1966 Waterford Town Guild
(committee member, Mrs Anne McCarthy)
weekly meeting notes:

Talks:
> How To Upholster A Small Stool;
> Smocked Cushion; Prevention Of Accidents
> To Children

Competitions:
> 'Most Songs With One Word In The Title';
> 1lb Marmalade; 'Prettiest Easter Bonnet
> From Paper'; 'A Shoulder Spray' 'A True
> Sponge'; 'A Light Fruit Cake'

Social half-hour:
> 'Embarrassing moments'; 'Ceili Dancing'
> 'Sing, Say, Or Something Pay'; Comic
> Knitting competition

Chapter One

*The Control Freak's Guide
to Pregnancy*

'I always wanted to have a baby. I just didn't know when I could fit one into my schedule.'

Pregnant woman in the *Sunday Times Magazine*, 2008

'Low spirits, violent passions, irritability, frivolity in the pregnant woman, leave indelible marks on the unborn child.'

From nineteenth-century childrearing guide *Safe Counsel*, in Ann Douglas, *You'll Spoil that Baby!: Vintage Baby and Childcare Advice*[1]

Ten, nearly eleven years ago, I was heavily pregnant with my first child, with a big red face and a bump so large it threatened to unbalance my small frame. My friends used to compare me to a Weeble, an egg-shaped toy popular in the 1970s which, when pushed, would wobble, but not fall over due to heavy weights in its bottom. 'Watch the Weeble wobble,' a friend of mine chortled when I visited her, eight months pregnant and like a ship about to set sail.

I eased my ample rear end onto her sofa and smiled at her beatifically and with more than a touch of the superior. What did she know? She was still single, whilst I was about to begin on the journey of a lifetime. I smugly clutched my bump, hardly able to contain my excitement at the prospect of seeing my baby for the first time. I was going to have a baby, I kept telling myself, a real, live *baby*.

What I had thought rather less about was that I was about to become a mother and what that might mean for me. My reaction to having a baby was entirely childlike, one of gleeful excitement at a wonderful surprise tempered not one bit by any sensible adult emotions, like responsibility. Motherhood, to me, was a fantasy of the kind I might see in a movie, or a Saturday-night drama: airbrushed, gorgeous, involving lots of love and cuddles, chats and play, in a substantial light-filled home. In the motherhood of my imagination there was no mess, no conflict, no anger, no depression, but a lifestyle-supplement, sun-filled picture of love and adoration of a tiny human being. As a mother I would resemble Caroline Ingalls from *Little House on the Prairie*, smiling, patient, gentle, ever vigilant to my child's needs – isn't that what mothers were? When I became a mother I would stop being me and metamorphose into that cardboard cut-out vision in my head and everything would be just fine.

Quite why I thought this, I'm not sure. After all, I had seen my own mother's struggle with motherhood, as the mother of three children, one of whom was autistic and who needed every ounce of care that she could muster. I had observed my friends' mothers – the sensible apron-clad older mothers of eight, brushing their kids out of the way to get on with the endless domestic tasks; the maxi-dress and headscarf-wearing, gin-drinking foxy younger mums who were the talk of the golf club; the nice, sensible mothers in their battered second cars, brown slacks and windcheaters out walking the dog – but when it came to motherhood, I couldn't see myself in them. In fact, I'm not entirely sure I could see myself as a mother at all.

However, what I did know, even as a little girl, was that motherhood was an *ideal*, not a mere job. And for us Catholic girls, the idea was fairly forced home that Holy Mary was It. She, after all, was the Mother of God, and there could be no higher aspiration than to emulate her maternal perfection, her patience, gentleness and forti- tude, in every way. Thus we competed furiously with our classmates to be the most fervent, the most religious, the most avid mutterer of Holy Marys and helpers of old ladies, many of whom were fairly niced to death by eager, pig-tail-wearing youngsters all offering to hold their shop- ping. For us, motherhood carried with it the faint whiff of martyrdom and self-sacrifice. And then the Irish Mammy was added into the mix, that fearsome specimen whose life depended on making her children's as comfort- able and hassle-free as possible; on grimly providing an endless succession of hot meals, clean clothes, ironed sheets, lifts to football practice, all of which ensured that her children – sons, generally, as girls were mercifully excused from such favouritism – would grow up into useless lumps whose status in society was guaranteed only by the fact that they were, well, men, whilst all those promising, bright, talented girls somehow fell away.

But when I sat on my friend's sofa, I had no idea of what lay ahead of me, that my smug certainties, my

Marian fantasies, would be turned on their heads and that having a baby, rather than being the pinnacle of my existence, another achievement to rank alongside getting married, buying a car and getting a promotion, was only the beginning of a much longer and more complex process. That motherhood wasn't a job at which I could excel simply by trying very, very hard to be like Holy Mary/Caroline Ingalls, but one which would shape me in all kinds of unexpected ways, which would reveal a side to me that I hardly knew existed. Over the next ten years I would hold a mirror up to myself and not always like what I saw, this ageing, saggy woman whose body had been scarred by pregnancy, whose mind was no longer her own and whose quixotic temper tantrums were far from the ideal of motherhood she had hoped for, but who would sometimes surprise herself with her resourcefulness and capabilities as a mother. During this time, I would experience rage, love, frustration, gloom to varying degrees, gut-wrenching feelings of inadequacy and overwhelming love and joy.

At the time, however, I simply felt that my bright-eyed optimism and my diligent preparation, and the saintly qualities I undoubtedly possessed, would carry me through. That loving it a lot would be all that was needed. And I had planned for and wanted this baby so much, after all. My chakras were in alignment, I had explored opportunities my mother and grandmother had only dreamed of. I smugly believed that because I was ready, well, everything would fall into place simply because I willed it to. After all, I was truly ready for this challenge.

*

One of the first things I would learn about motherhood is that I wouldn't get what I wanted, simply because I really, *really* wanted it. We are conditioned to believe that because we strive and work hard for something, we somehow deserve it. Motherhood is our right, rather than our privilege.

Only now, talking to my mother, do I feel gratitude for this right, to be complacent about having children, the right to the Will-I, Won't-I dithering that now accompanies the decision to have a baby. Throughout my twenties, I had felt darts of broodiness as the possibility of having a family of my own became slowly more real. Wistfully, I would wonder if the timing was right, uhming and awing, trying to put my biological urge to have a baby to one side to focus on my career, on doing all the things I felt I should do before a baby would put a stop to life as I knew it.

For Nana and Mum, there literally was no choice. Marriage and children went together. The idea that there was a 'right time' to have children wasn't even considered. You got married, had children and got on with it, as my mother told me. 'It was expected of us to have a baby in the first year of marriage and if you didn't, there was something wrong with you. Surely what else would you get married for, but to have children?'

What's more, in Ireland, the Church's ruling on contraception was draconian – all artificial contraception was banned until the 1970s and many couples went along with it, whether they liked it or not. Children just arrived, one after another, and the parents had little choice in the matter, as one bewildered Cork woman remarked in a book on local women's experiences: 'Years went by and the babies arrived at an alarming rate.'[2]

I was quite chuffed to discover that during the time when Ireland was in the iron grip of the Catholic Church my grandparents had formed a kind of French Resistance of contraception, supplying local couples in Arklow with marital gold dust in the form of a book on contraception by a certain Halliday G. Sutherland. This book contained information on the safe and fertile periods, and in spite of its entirely mild advice, was banned by the notorious Censorship Board, following the dictates of the Church who, although they couldn't find anything in the safe period that contradicted Catholic teaching, knew that it was definitely Not a Good Thing.[3] By some means my

2. Source: Eileen Moon, quoting her mother, Fran McCarthy in 'A Woman of Substance', a booklet produced for International Women's Day by the Cork Federation of Women's Organisations, 1994.

3. Source: *The Slow Failure: Population Decline and Independent Ireland, 1920–73*, Mary E. Daly, University of Wisconsin Press, 2006

grandparents had got hold of a copy of the lethal book, and when word got out, a succession of anxious people turned up on their doorstep to be solemnly handed the explosive reading material in a brown paper bag.

My grandparents were good Catholics, but were not as awed by the Church as they might have been; as a well-paid civil servant, earning between three and six pounds per week, Granddad was secure enough in his job to defy the powers that were. Thirty years later, in spite of the swinging Sixties, my own parents would be obedient to the dictates of their religion, which outlawed all artificial forms of contraception, as my mother ruefully explained: 'Well, the Pill was available, but you'd have to smuggle it in from England, and that was only done by louche, arty people.' But when the fact that my brother had learning difficulties became very apparent, and with a small baby – me – now in tow, my mother knew that she couldn't cope with any more children and asked her doctor for help. And even though the Pill was then legally available in certain circumstances, her request was denied by her conservative doctor, with a pat on the shoulder and a 'There, there.' 'Social' rather than medical reasons, in his view, didn't merit the Pill.

Like so many women at the time, my mother was angry, but stoic. Her weekly Mass attendance did not falter, even as the priests ranted and raved from the pulpit about corrupt morals: 'I didn't pray for the Pope's Intentions any more, though,' she admitted, explaining why she no longer followed the priest's invitation to pray for his Holiness' concerns of the moment, 'as his intentions weren't very good.'

As soon as the law was changed to allow contraception for married couples in all circumstances, my mother marched off to the family planning clinic in a basement in a leafy Dublin street and was issued her prescription by the lovely sensible ladies who worked there. At last, as a married woman in her thirties, my mother was able to control her own destiny.

I grew up at the tail end of the Church-run state in Ireland, when it was still difficult to get hold of contraception – condoms were only legalized when I was seventeen – and when any discussion of sex was surrounded by vague obfuscation and downright misinformation. In my secondary school Mother Mary-Joseph was chief among the misinformers, conducting several ad-hoc 'sex education' classes when she should have been taking second-year musicianship, which consisted of her advising us on no account to wear patent-leather shoes as 'he' – for which read the man, i.e. devil child/Satan/Beelzebub – would be able to see your knickers, and something else to do with putting a telephone directory on a boy's knee before you sat on it, the better to resist any unholy impulses, which actually sounds quite forward, when you think about it. Quite frankly, most of us had never heard the word 'vagina', and only 'penis' because bold Fidelma in Year Three blurted it out during double maths to see if

Sister Attracta was paying attention or if she'd fallen asleep again over trigonometry.

But the rapidity with which we threw out our bleak Catholic inheritance was surprising. We got the hang of sex in spite of the efforts of Mother Mary-Joseph, and as soon as we could get hold of contraception we marched forward into modernity with barely a look back at our past.

Thus, when I was twenty-five, I still indulged in the mildest bit of Catholic guilt about postponing a family, I couldn't even imagine what it would be like not to be able to control my own life and, most importantly, when I chose to have a baby. Thanks to my mother, who considered marriage carefully because she knew that an immediate family was a given, I had the great privilege to be able to wait. And so, I waited.

And when I was thirty, it all fell into place, just as I had planned. One minute I was hanging out in jazz clubs in a down-at-heel-but-trendy part of North London, the next I was examining babygros in Mothercare. My baby was due on 4 July and I immediately began to consult the pregnancy oracles and take massive amounts of antenatal vitamins. My body would be a temple, I decided, and every step of my pregnancy would be monitored closely. Life was slotting so perfectly into place and my dreams of starting a family were about to come true.

But of course, nature had other ideas. When I miscarried at just under twelve weeks, I blamed myself. After all, I had discovered that I was pregnant only after an epic binge at a wedding where I had smoked untold cigarettes and drunk far too many piña coladas. So it was all my fault, wasn't it? The fact that I had treated my body like a temple after that was only window-dressing. I was devastated and felt deeply guilty and no amount of hearty midwives telling me that these things happen, particularly in first pregnancies, could cheer me up. I simply hadn't envisioned failure of any kind and the mild physical humiliation that followed was chastening, the poking and the prodding, the sticking of things up my rear end, the necessity of having an 'ERPC', which chilling acronym actually means Evacuation of Retained Products of Conception, a term to upset even the most hardened individual.

I waited for seven hours to be told what I already knew in an overcrowded Accident and Emergency department in London, surrounded by drunken people and miserable-looking individuals with bandaged limbs. The hospital doctor was mortified as he hadn't wanted to examine me, but we'd all given up on the gynaecologist after the half-day's wait. He wasn't sure, he said sheepishly, I'd need a scan to confirm. I looked at him bleakly and gathered my stuff, my unfinished novel – unread, needless to say – and bumper pack of tissues, grabbed the scan appointment form and shuffled out the door, breathing in the chill December air with relief, the noise and the bustle, the normality of the street after the stuffy, recycled air and muted misery of the hospital. Unable to take in what was happening, my husband and I decided to get something to eat and we had a beer and a pizza in Pizza Express, like a normal couple out on a Friday night, even though our world had turned on its axis. Like a pair of eejits we sat there, politely chewing our pizza. 'It happens to lots of people,' I said brightly. Yes, my husband agreed. And this wasn't the end of the road, was it? We'd try again.

A further scan confirmed the miscarriage and I was handed a pink form and a hospital appointment for my ERPC, in a women's hospital I'd never heard of before, the medical equivalent of a Siberian Gulag, obscure, shadowy, the ward entirely silent and filled with miserable couples like us, all waiting for the finality of the procedure. Conversation was murmured, punctuated by silence and sighing. I was put to sleep by a bracing elderly Indian lady anaesthetist with a long grey plait down her back, telling me cheerfully: 'I'm going to stick a tablet up your bum now!' When I awoke in the recovery area, the consultant came to see me and told me that I had had a 'missed' miscarriage and that whilst my baby had died at nine weeks or so, my body hadn't realized and had kept on thinking it was pregnant for another couple of weeks. How stupid could my body be, I wondered – wasn't I supposed to be at one with nature and all that? I discovered that I couldn't control my pregnancy, that nature was boss here and she called the shots. It was a humbling experience. I could want a baby all I liked, but I wouldn't necessarily get one.

An hour later, my husband and I were back on the 73 bus to Islington. And it was really only afterwards that it began to sink in, that we had lost not just a dream, but a person. When I look at one of my children now, heads bent over the copybook, humming away to themselves as they cut and stick, or absorbed in *The Simpsons*, I sometimes wonder who this other person, this shadow baby, might have been.

When I was growing up, I was dimly aware, in the disinterested, self-absorbed way that children are, that Nana had lost four babies. The actual facts were shrouded in mystery and in the unreliability of memory, and of course, when Nana spoke about it, I only half-listened to her. I had no real idea what she was saying, how and when she had 'lost' them and what it really meant as she burbled on about how Jack hadn't wanted to adopt as adopted children caused their parents no end of trouble. I murmured in teenage half-sympathy, unable to work out what response was required of me.

Of course, it was only later, as a mother myself and with a bit of adult compassion in my soul, that I came to understand. For me, losing one baby was heartbreaking, difficult, undignified, but almost forgotten in the excitement and possibility of a new, happy, problem-free pregnancy and the birth of my son. But to lose four babies, to endure the mystifying and futile process of 'lying up' for the best part of a year, of hospital visits and doctors shaking their heads in puzzlement, only for them to end in tragedy is unimaginable. And all for the simple reason that Nana's Rhesus Negative blood group was incompatible with her babies', a problem which is solved nowadays with a single injection. For my mother, the miracle baby who was spared, Nana's pregnancies meant long absences from her, and regular visits to Arklow from her Granny MacNeill to mind her, but for Nana it meant hope and then failure, her only keepsake two death certificates from the babies who had made it far enough to be termed 'stillborn', and what I now realize must have been profound grief.

Compared to what Nana must have endured, my reaction to my miscarriage seems like the utmost in self-absorption, and yet nowadays losing babies is no longer part of our expectations in the Western world. Unlike in Nana's day, when children, if they made it out into the world, risked death from scarlet fever or diphtheria, we march forward, confident in the expectation of success, that nature won't punch us in the heart more than once, surely?

It took me – us – a full nine months to pluck up the courage to take the risk a second time. I was afraid that my body might fail again at this most natural of tasks, but more importantly, that I might have to lose another little person in my life. The prospect seemed almost too much to bear. And so, when I found myself pregnant again I held my breath for three months – I'm surprised the baby wasn't blue when he emerged. I did a lot of lying down, and refused to do my thrice-weekly swim, or to do anything other than walk up and down the stairs, to lie prone in front of the television and spend a lot of time asleep. And although this might sound like New Age mumbo-jumbo, I kind of knew at an elemental level that this pregnancy would be OK: the person who nestled inside seemed to have a firmer grip, a stronger toe-hold on life, and the pregnancy felt more 'real'. I could barely tolerate smells: the daily bus journey on the stuffy Routemaster bus with all the windows closed was an obstacle course of BO and stale cigarette smoke, which made me retch; I found that the only things I enjoyed eating were bananas and digestive biscuits and I retained enough wind to power the National Grid. This promised to be a pregnancy of epic flatulence. But also, I was physically in much better shape: I had given up smoking – properly – hadn't had a drink in months and had taken folic acid for the required weeks before-hand. My body really was a temple. I tried hard not to wonder if I had been more careful the first time . . . and attempted instead to look forward to the whole new life that awaited me.

I was in luck: an early scan revealed a tiny jumping bean bobbing up and down in the void, a heartbeat thumping away vigorously. I knew that it would be all right. My husband and I realized that, once more, we could hope and expect and look forward to the future we both so wanted. The irony was that I swung immediately into full control-freak mode once more. Had I learned nothing? Well, yes, that I was in the process of something outside myself, bigger, more mysterious and capricious than I had imagined, but you know what, I would conquer it. So, the pregnancy books were dug out from under the sofa, an extra-large bottle of Gaviscon indigestion remedy was purchased, the scans were booked. I fussed about blood tests and amniocentesis and cot sizes and scratch mittens. I started pondering my birth plan at twelve weeks, wondering whether or not I'd have an epidural, whatever the hell that was, and if a birth pool would be good, of course having no clue what the whole business might actually entail. This pregnancy and the subsequent birth would resemble the assault on El Alamein in the sheer scale and precision of its planning.

Unlike Mum and Nana, I couldn't be bothered with old wives' lore about never drinking Coke in case it would turn the baby yellow, or about turning the baby if it was breech by walking around an oak tree nine times. I knew better: the books would tell me all that I needed to know. So what if the chemist had to shout at me, as I mumbled a request for Preparation H, 'Is it the piles, love, they're awful in pregnancy, aren't they?' I hadn't read that in 'Chapter 2: Your Growing Baby'; it told me everything I needed to know about the development of the foetus and about blood tests and haemoglobin levels, but not about practical stuff like piles, and the way my feet would grow another size and my hair would fall out and some of my teeth would get wobbly. 'Oh, yes,' my mother said darkly when I reported this phenomenon to her, 'you lose a tooth with each baby.' In my case, my mother and her sage advice had been replaced by *What to Expect When You're Expecting*, common sense had been replaced by science.

*

As a bewildered, sheeplike pregnant woman I had to negotiate the schism between the firm-busted-midwife and the grumpy-obstetrician schools of antenatal care and childbirth, unsure of which to follow, whether to trust my instincts as a pregnant woman or to accept all that science had to offer, all those lovely reassuring scans and tests, which would demonstrate to me what I may, or may not, have needed to know.

In the shiny new modern Ireland of 1963, my mother was able to avail herself of the free antenatal care that had eventually been introduced after the customary tussle with the Catholic Church[4] and to choose one of the best

4. In 1951, the then Minister for Health, Dr Noel Browne, had introduced a scheme whereby all pregnant women could avail themselves of free antenatal care. Disturbed at what they saw as the unnecessary meddling in family life by the state, the Church decided to meddle instead, making its disapproval of the scheme clear, on the grounds that parents should decide what kind of care they needed, not the state. They succeeded in scuppering

obstetricians in the country to supervise her pregnancy and the birth of her first child, which would take place in one of the city's big maternity hospitals. She had insisted on a hospital birth, because, as she admitted to me, 'I felt so nervous of the birth and I felt all along that I wasn't cut out for natural childbirth.' My mother was brave enough to admit to feelings all expectant mothers share about the realities of childbirth – which one of us wouldn't honestly like to be hit over the head well before the onset of labour and to be presented with a baby only when we have come to? – but in Mum's day, childbirth was dangerous. My father's mother had died in childbirth, Nana had lost several babies and now here my mother was – a doctor-supervised pregnancy in a hospital offered the possibility of lowering the danger odds.

When I had my son almost forty years later, my antenatal care was provided by a lovely group of midwives in a busy London clinic, one of half a dozen or so satellites of the large teaching hospital which I had chosen for the birth. (When I say 'chosen', I never really thought of an alternative. You had babies in hospital, didn't you?) I attended the midwives' clinic because that was what you did – antenatal care in England was provided thus, unless you wanted to pay for the Rolls-Royce option and head for the exclusive hushed portals of the consultant's waiting

---

the plan but ironically, a modified version of the scheme would be introduced a few years later, from which my mother benefited.

rooms, or were unlucky enough to have a complicated pregnancy, which required specialist care.

For five months the lovely ladies weighed and measured me and chatted happily to me about wind and constipation – mine, not theirs – and what I was going to call the baby. 'Have we weed onto the stick, Alison?' they would gently chide me, as they tested my blood pressure and asked me if I'd had any peculiar symptoms – well . . . I thought ruefully as I examined my swelling belly which grumbled and creaked and groaned like a shipwreck, feeling like a giant walking, breathing symptom. They swished their magic wands over my stomach so we could hear the baby's heartbeat and although they must have listened to hundred of heartbeats, they would always smile broadly when they heard the gentle *swoosh*, *swoosh* confirming that all was well. The midwives were a fount of wisdom and gentle reassurance and patience at my antenatal worries and grumbles and ensured that my pregnancy was as serene and 'normal' as any panicky first mother's could be.

The irony was that during my mother's pregnancy, which was a difficult one, marked by high blood pressure and wretched morning sickness, she didn't receive the sympathetic ear she wanted, nor were her worries taken seriously. In August and September 1963, when she would have been five or six months pregnant, there was so little movement from the baby that Mum visited her consultant in a panic, who patted her gently on the hand

and reassured her that 'all will be well, my dear, you're just having a baby'. 'I had the feeling that all was not well,' she told me, but with no scans available to indicate otherwise, Mum was forced to keep her worries to herself. And her mother was no help, my mother's every statement greeted with portentous doom by Nana, for understandable reasons. ' "Uhm," was all I ever heard,' my mother tells me. 'It was all bound up with her own feelings.'

*

When I returned to Ireland and was pregnant with my second child, I found it interesting that the medicalization of childbirth which took place in my mother's time persists to this day, with many of my friends and relatives opting to spend several thousand euro on the childbirth package that comes with our health insurance, and the weekly scans, reassuring words from a tweed-suited individual with a novelty tie, and the ultimate in sophisticated childbirth: the promise of his/her presence during the labour and birth, which really separates the plebs from the gentry. 'Just to be on the safe side,' a friend of mine said when I asked her about her decision. Safe from what I wondered, muttering darkly about pregnancy not being a disease.

Used as I was to the firm-busted reassurance of the midwives' clinic, my first antenatal visit to a Dublin maternity hospital was a rude awakening. The waiting room resembled the deck of the *Titanic*, an overheated cacophony of disgruntled pregnant women and their young children, shrieking with boredom. I could hardly believe my eyes – all of these women, and there must have been a couple of hundred of them, were here to see one consultant obstetrician. After an hour on the wreck of the Hesperus, my name was called and I was ushered into the consultant's office, there to be treated to a grilling by a rather grumpy whey-faced man with a spectacular comb-over, who displayed minimal interest in me or my pregnancy – I wondered if I should ask him whether he'd like to dispense with the consultation altogether and simply affix a bright yellow tag to my ear and brand my backside with the logo of the hospital.

Feeling just like the cow I so obviously was, I marched up to the receptionist's desk and cleared my throat. The girl with the Croydon facelift looked up from her nail-filing for a moment. 'Yeah?'

'I was wondering if I could see a midwife, or is the doctor the only option?' I enquired politely.

Croydon Facelift looked at me as if I had asked for a Voodoo witch who would slice open a hen's neck and scatter blood all over my pregnant belly. 'A *midwife?* Well, yeah,' she reluctantly admitted. Croydon pointed a finger in the direction of the shaman's cave, in the office just next to the consultant, with a queue of precisely one pregnant woman waiting outside.

I was delighted to return to the certainties of my

lovely lady friends and their gentle questioning about weeing and putting my feet up. Here were women who actually cared about me and my baby and enjoyed a little comforting chat over the urine sample, whereupon I would leave feeling buoyed up and ready for action. And I could be assured of continuity of care: that one of these lovely ladies whom I had come to know over the course of my pregnancy would be present at the birth of my child.

I was surprised, however, at others' reaction to my choice of a midwife rather than an obstetrician – that I was a bit of a hippy, trusting in old wives' lore when surely I should know that the answers lay in science. Some even led me to believe that I was somehow negligent of my baby, unwilling to spend the kind of money that would ensure the *absolute safety* of my unborn child. Sometimes I even doubted my own instincts, that unless there were complications in my pregnancy – and there never were, mercifully – I wasn't actually ill; that weekly scans would tell me – well, nothing really, at least nothing that I could do anything about, but would instead induce a level of unnecessary hysteria; that sometimes the antenatal tests caused worry and stress for no reason, leaving me constantly wondering if I was about to be told that the baby had some life-threatening illness every time I stepped over the threshold of the hospital.

It seemed to me that the proper medical care which was so essential to the survival of pregnant women and children in Ireland a hundred years ago had become for many the *only* way to care for mothers and babies; at least, the only 'proper' way, with the average pregnancy and birth increasingly coming to be seen by some women as 'dangerous', which might explain why some opted for certainty in what is, after all, a 'natural' process. But I was equally fascinated by why other women chose to turn their backs on medicine altogether and to swim in what many might consider the 'dangerous' waters of natural pregnancy and birth, trusting in Maya chanting and Hopi Indian remedies and the kind of New Age stuff that made other mothers' hair stand on end. In my pregnancies, I fell somewhere in between. It seemed to me that 'hospi-talization' of pregnancy had turned everything on its head – that it was assumed everything was wrong until it was proven otherwise. With the midwives, I felt it to be the opposite – everything would be fine, unless there was firm evidence to the contrary. I was not a fan of going through pregnancy on a cloud of patchouli, wafting along, hairy armpits aloft, ignoring any of the opportunities for reassurance and, crucially, the lifesaving possibilities of science, but where a pregnancy is normal, I felt I could trust in the centuries-old experience, the advice and support of the trained midwife.

And, I suppose, somewhere at the back of my mind, were stored the difficult conversations I had had with my mother as soon as I was old enough to hear the trauma of my brother's birth, of her deep anger at the neglect she felt she experienced at the hands of the staff at the hospital, at the blame she placed on them for what happened to my brother. Subconsciously, perhaps I felt that doctors wouldn't give me the support and reassurance I was looking for.

*

But that didn't mean that I would approach the birth of my child without the maximum preparation, without being armed to the teeth with the information that I felt would ward off any untoward happenings. Information, and the deluge thereof, has become the Maya Chanting of the twenty-first-century woman. In my case, knowing *everything I could* about my pregnancy and birth gave me a welcome sense of control at a thoroughly mystifying time in my life.

In my pregnancy my body had become a stranger to me, having taken on a life of its own, swelling, leaking and sprouting as the months progressed. My stomach seemed to inflate at the very idea of the baby, making my pregnancy visible at an unwelcomely early juncture; it became a little gaseous balloon making way for its still-tiny passenger; after my regular swim, I would be doubled up in pain which, when I consulted the pregnancy oracle, I was informed was the 'soft ligaments' of my stomach stretching, which all sounded rather alarming. There were the aforementioned piles about which nothing further needs to be said, there were the blinding headaches, which I'd never had before in my life, there was the allergy to any kind of smell – the rush of nausea that greeted a whiff of someone else's smelly armpits or cheese sandwiches. I had the growing sense that my body was doing what it wanted and needed to do, regardless of whether I liked it or not. You'd think that as women we might be prepared for this, have had some inkling that our bodies might not be under our control at some time in the future, and yet I found the process rather like jumping out of an aeroplane – exhilarating and terrifying at the same time.

I know that some women loathe their pregnancies, are plagued by fatigue and nausea and general discomfort, but I was one of those unpleasantly smug individuals who 'glowed'; who found new reserves of energy as the second trimester came, who bounced along with rosy cheeks and shiny hair – pregnancy really suited me and, anxiety notwithstanding, I had such an easy time of it physically. I gained little weight in spite of eating enough to feed half of North London and I loved the growing sense of a real person inside me: the excitement of feeling a fluttering like butterflies in my stomach for the first time, and then a tiny movement in my stomach, which, as the months wore on, became a series of bumps and wriggles, flying elbows and knees, sometimes quite alarmingly active, a watchful presence startled by sudden noise or loud music, lulled by movement, alarmed by cold drinks or any agitation on my part.

I was exhilarated, but also terrified at the changes taking place. Reading pregnancy manuals helped me to make sense of these changes, to anchor them in a series of quantifiables – in four-week stages of growth and development, in trimesters, the wretched first, followed by the glowing second and, finally, the weary third.

My easy pregnancy came as a relief, because in my 'other' life, outside my pregnancy, I was completely lost. After two miserable years in a groovy London publisher, it was brought to my attention that I was totally unsuited to the ascetic life of a literary editor and I found myself, to my shock and dismay, pregnant and jobless. I continued to pretend that life was relatively normal, the only comfort for my loss of identity and status the reasonably substantial cheque I now clutched in my hot and sticky hands and the fact that during the next year I would have the baby I so wanted.

Unlike my mother, who would have expected to make the transition to motherhood without fuss, there being no other option, I had worked steadily for ten years before becoming pregnant, I had had all the fun to which I felt I was entitled, so I felt annihilated by the loss of my job: at that stage my identity was completely bound up with what I did – I am an editor therefore I am – and motherhood had not yet come along to show me that there were alternatives.

And so even though, unlike Mum, my pregnancy was an easy one, I spent most of the next six months leading up to the birth of my baby in a state of complete panic, unable to sleep at night, unsure of what the future held, trying to cling onto small comforts: the purchasing of my not-exactly-dream home in Stoke Newington from a very pleasant West Indian man, which came complete with a gigantic fish tank housing one solitary piranha and several Polish people in the attic – when we had come to view the house, we had interrupted one girl and her mother holding a chicken over the flame of a portable stove – the purchasing of substantial amounts of baby gear; and manic fussing over inflammable mattresses and sterilizing sets. I edited books as usual, now as a freelancer, gritting my teeth over prepositions and split infinitives, wondering whether the travel book by an elderly and cantankerous author needed quite so much detail on the wild goats of Afghanistan; I wrote the opening chapters of a novel in which a Londoner is shot dead in mysterious circumstances at his local swimming pool, because I like swimming; I attempted to learn to drive. I *was* going to regain control of my life, I thought, as I careered around the narrow streets of Hackney in a Nissan Micra, a worried-looking lady instructor in the seat beside me, urging me to 'Try second gear, dear.' 'You drive the car, the car doesn't drive you,' Audrey would occasionally remind me gently – a metaphor if ever there was one.

It was at my antenatal classes, conducted by a slightly scary but very warm former midwife, that I found a reassuring anchor for the rest of my pregnancy and also a supportive group of friends who didn't blanch visibly, or murmur 'unclean' when I mentioned my jobless status, and who would become essential to me in the early days of my son's life. In the spirit of Maximum Preparation, I had decided to pay privately for the classes, as the rushed, scanty ones of the hospital seemed somehow inadequate, and I felt a pressing need to put a shape on the unknowable. I was referred to Slightly Scary Brenda by the brusque woman at the Association of Bossy Maternity Professionals, and only after she had expressed the appropriate amount of horror and disappointment at me having left it so late. 'Of course all the classes are booked!' she shrieked, implying that only a negligent person would think otherwise. Thankfully, Brenda's response was a crisp, businesslike invite to the next scheduled class. On the first night, six couples sat on scatter cushions on the floor of her lovely Victorian home, waiting for the secrets of the Holy Grail to be revealed.

My need to conquer the unforeseen with knowledge, to regain control over the chaos of my life, is in stark contrast to my mother's more relaxed approach. Knocked out by the medication she was taking to control her high blood pressure, she would spend much of the time asleep on her feet and the rest of the time diligently reading up on the subject of pregnancy and childbirth from a range of sources, including magazines like *Woman's Life*, where the advice came interspersed with ads for ironing boards – 'perfect for the wife just returned from honeymoon!' –

detailed knitting patterns for children's jumpers and 'ten tips for nice nails'. 'Your father was off every day doing his thing and there was nobody around to talk to and so I read about pregnancy and labour in magazines and books.' What's clear is that my mother was not a fan of the natural childbirth extolled in the newfangled antenatal classes which were being introduced at the time: 'Oh, I didn't attend those relaxation classes. I said, "I'm not an African and I don't want to squat over a hole to deliver the baby,"' she told me, oblivious to my snorts of laughter.

She would have been vaguely mortified at the hang-loose, encounter-group spirit of Brenda's antenatal class, where over the course of six weeks or so we talked about our feelings and what our expectations of childbirth were, as well as in forensic detail about what the process actually involved. We discussed our perineums – or perinea – did we know where it was, Brenda enquired? No, we did not, never having had any use for it until now. Had we done our pelvic floor exercises, a hundred squeezes and releases umpteen times a day? (An Irish friend of mine living in London at the time spent one frantic week after her antenatal class wondering what her 'pelvic flaw' could be – what was wrong with her pelvis anyway?)

'When you are hanging out the washing, or climbing the stairs, just stop for a moment and squeeze and release,' Brenda advised. I am sure my neighbours wondered why I would pause at the washing line or on the stairs to my flat, transfixed, before marching onwards, a satisfied look on my face. My pelvic floor became the centre of my life.

Of course, when it came to the Thing That Dare Not Speak Its Name – i.e. The Birth – we might as well have been talking about how we would enjoy a lunar landing, so remote did it all seem. When we reached that part of the antenatal classes, Brenda matter-of-factly produced a plastic pelvis from behind the chintz-covered sofa and pushed a small doll into it, imitating the twists and turns of the 'real baby'. We looked on, bemused – it felt like a fifth-year biology class. Then, equally matter-of-factly, she acted out a 'typical' labour for us, pushing and panting and oohing and aahing through contractions, then the drama of the second stage, with the pushing now accompanied by equally demure moans. 'Oh, here's the baby and . . . aah,' she breathed, a transfixed look on her face. We looked at her silently, with the same mixture of fascination and faint embarrassment that greets someone doing a limbo dance or one of those Indian mystics who hang water-filled bottles from their testicles. It was as if we were witnessing some intimate act. We left the class quietly preoccupied with the momentous event which awaited us and slightly shocked that it might actually be this, well, *physical*.

I now think that the reason we got so exercised about the birth process – the birth canal and forceps deliveries, Caesarean versus natural births, the blessed perinea and pelvic floors — was because what lay beyond was so mysterious and difficult, so unknown, that it was terrain that could not even be contemplated. So instead we focused on getting our birth experiences just right. I approached my first and second stages, my panting and my breathing, as if it were an exam. My birth plan was my thesis: a twelve-point manifesto for how I envisioned the birth of my child, full of terms like 'I would like not to have an episiotomy' — well, who the hell would?; and 'I would like to listen to the attached CD of whale music'; and 'I would like to push for precisely half an hour, panting every three to four minutes'. I felt that by organizing myself, my thoughts and the trajectory of my birth experience, *I* would be in charge.

Take It from Me

* Before you have your first baby you look pityingly at other mothers-to-be, huffing and puffing up the road, swigging from a large-size bottle of Gaviscon like a wino with a two-litre flagon of cider; and the unkempt new mums with straggly hair and, gasp, stains on their T-shirts, and think that you will be different. You won't end up a greasy-haired, tracksuited version of your former self, you snort. Unlike every other mother that has gone before you, you will have a glorious pregnancy in which your hair

will be shiny, your clothes will be carefully chosen,
you will be pile- and heartburn-free. And when you
have your baby, you won't need an epidural, but will
waft him/her out in your birthing pool, and then
you'll breastfeed, wash your hair, prepare a three-
course meal for your beloved and perfect a new
sexual position, all whilst putting several loads in the
machine and hoovering the dust from underneath the
bed. Well, you know what, you won't. Because you
are human, and you don't have access to a twenty-
four-hour on-call personal trainer, nurse, and posse of
beauticians to keep things on track, and those beatific
women in the celebrity magazines are just there to
taunt you; you will be affected by your pregnancy,
by the ravages of childbirth, and when baby arrives,
you'll be lucky to be able to brush your teeth. Sorry,
but that's the truth. So be kind to yourself and avert
your eyes when some sickening TV presenter/celeb
appears on the front of *OK* with a new set of boobs
and a taut tummy just days after giving birth to little
Tarquin – it's not real, and it's not healthy. Have
another chocolate biscuit and curl up on the sofa with
your bump and a good book – it is the only time in
your entire life that you will be able to do this.

* Try not to succumb to status one-upmanship when
  it comes to preparing for the arrival of your precious
  bundle. Your baby will not give a rat's ass, if you'll

pardon the expression, what clothes you are putting on him, or where you change his/her little bottom or what you push him up and down the road in, so don't beat yourself up if you haven't got the status baby-carrier of the moment, or if you don't live in a five-bedroom house set on several acres of rolling farmland because it'd give you more room for his playgym and treehouse – he or she will not be scanning the living room for evidence of naff decorative taste, aged two weeks.

* People react to pregnancy in different ways: some decide that they absolutely have to hang-glide off Everest as they may never get the opportunity again, others lie on the sofa until D-Day, watching *EastEnders*. As long as you are not doing anything illegal, that's fine. You will know what you are capable of – but no heavy lifting. I have seen heavily pregnant women attempting to heave huge suitcases around or propping their six-year-old up on their bump and find it hard to resist the urge to shriek, 'Stop!' Life is not a competition, so ask someone to help you.

* In my antenatal yoga class, a woman confessed to being obsessed with black pudding, which the teacher told her was just fine, but when she went on to say that coal looked utterly tempting, the teacher

suggested she see her GP. You will find yourself
assaulted with a battery of conflicting advice on what
to eat/not eat/drink/not drink during your
pregnancy. Try to be sensible, whilst not getting into
too much of a sweat about it, but seek advice if non-
food items look appealing. Similarly, the advice about
what to eat or not eat during pregnancy changes
regularly: I have eaten pounds of tuna, only to
discover after the fact that my youngest's brain was
now full of mercury, because I hadn't read the edict
on not eating seafood in pregnancy. A reasonable
balance is the wisest approach, I feel, and stockpile
the runny cheese for after the birth.

* Listen to, and respect, your mother in your pregnancy
if you have a reasonable relationship with her. She
may have had a baby thirty years ago, but she had one
and probably in more difficult circumstances than you
will have to face, so give her a break. Even if you
think she's talking utter nonsense, nod your head and
look interested – she's remembering her own
experiences at this special time for you.

* Many people wonder why there are no books on
miscarriage, but I know I certainly didn't want to
read one – it would not have helped me understand
why I lost my first pregnancy or helped me onwards
to the next one because there was no explanation for

what had happened. Nature ensures that we mourn and then try again and unless there is a recurring medical situation, that's what we will do. But conversations with many other women will reveal that you are not alone, that many others have gone through the same thing. Perhaps you wish that people were more open about it, but pregnancy and birth is a land of secrets, of things that no-one tells you, which remain hidden, sometimes for entirely appropriate reasons.

Chapter Two

Voyage into the Unknown:
the Birth 'Experience'

'Even the pangs which, since the Fall, the mother must suffer in order to bring forth her child, serve but to draw ever closer the bond that unites them; the more pain the child will cost her, the greater her love for it.'

'In the Service of Life'; address delivered by his Holiness Pope Pius XII to the Congress of the Catholic Union of Midwives, Oct 1951

'Childbirth, however transcendent or revelatory it may or may not be, still hurts like hell.'

Susan Maushart, *The Mask of Motherhood*, (Penguin, 1999)

In the last few days of my pregnancies, time slowed almost to a standstill; a hush seemed to fall as I entered a dreamlike state, propped up on the sofa, shuffling to the kitchen and back, or in bed late at night unable to sleep; the baby's movements slowed, too, as the space left for wriggling and kicking had shrunk and as it headed for the departure lounge. It was as if the two of us were suspended in a bubble, between one world and the next. We both waited quietly and watchfully for life to change for ever.

I was over the weariness of the last few weeks of pregnancy – the bladder-bashing, rib-kicking sleeplessness, the feeling that I had a bag of cement strapped to my stomach, the weariness of heaving my reluctant body on and off the bus to work, the indignity and mystery of the antenatal appointments, with the poking and prodding, the urine samples and the blood pressure gauges, the gnomic pronouncements of the medical professionals, the pain of heartburn, the manic cleaning of the kitchen and forensic examination of the fridge for evidence of lurking bacteria, the nest-building surge of energy that came before the final few days and which saw me cleaning the toilet cistern and opening the back of the television, the better to remove any dust that might alarm my newborn.

I had got over the frustration of wanting the baby to arrive *right now* so that I could stop being pregnant, just for a little bit. But the weariness and fatigue were now replaced by a curious vertigo, a lack of certainty, a mixture of trepidation and excitement about this voyage into the unknown, this journey that everyone told me would change everything but in ways I couldn't foresee. Your life will never be the same, other parents told me, but *how*, I wondered. What is it they knew that I didn't? What was that wary look in their eyes when I gushed about how fulfilling my life would be once I had a baby, how I couldn't wait to hold my baby, to show him/her off, to feed, care, cuddle and nurture this little person, to become a *Mother*? Sure, others told me that I didn't know what I was letting myself in for, with a wry look on their faces, but isn't having a baby one of life's miracles? And hadn't I prepared for it over the last nine months: the carefully selected baby gear, the reading of pregnancy books until they fell apart from over-use, the eight antenatal classes, the forty-point birth plan, a list which I hoped would cover every eventuality in this mysterious process, this voyage into the unknown.

I sensed the enormity of the change ahead, but couldn't quite get any shape on it and so I clung to certainties like a drowning man to driftwood: the birth plan, the final midwife visit where I learned that the baby was 'engaged' and that it was only a question of time now. I rang my oldest friend, who was also having a baby, and we both laughed about pregnancy's indignities. I hinted at my nerves to this mother-of-two, who in the tradition of mothers from time immemorial, gave nothing away other than vague soothing generalities – in the same way as I would when I had children and was faced with the rabbit-in-the-headlights questions of first-time mothers.

The day before my baby was due, I met a friend at a local café who'd just had a baby. I gurgled and made faces at her gorgeous baby whilst my friend shyly confessed to having 'absolutely needed' an epidural. 'Oh, the pain,' she sighed. I nodded abstractly, ignorant of what she was obliquely trying to share with me.

'And I dirtied the sheets,' she confessed.

I smiled blithely, cradling my bump: 'Well, there can be blood loss, I suppose. Isn't that part of labour?'

'No, I mean, well, poo.' I was horrified and mildly revolted. Could she not have restrained herself? And what had poo got to do with having a baby anyway – the books didn't say anything about it, not in the careful descriptions of dilation and waters breaking. Well, when I had my baby, I thought to myself, I wouldn't make a holy show of myself like she had.

I returned home from this encounter none the wiser about the realities of having a baby and flapped a bit and wondered what I should do now – should I go for a swim, another walk, watch *Friends* on a loop, as others told me I'd never watch television again, so profoundly would my life change. Everything seemed so banal, so ordinary, with the people rushing by on their way to work, home and supermarket, when I was on the verge of something extraordinary. And so I waited, suspended between two worlds, for my life to change for ever.

*

When my waters broke in the middle of the night, I remember looking at the puddle on the bathroom floor and thinking a lot of things. Had I, in fact, weed on the floor, had my body done something strange and unexpected yet again? What should I do now? Wait a bit, ring the hospital, wake my husband up? Bizarrely, my mind flicked back to a conversation with a friend in which she had assured me that women whose waters broke in Marks & Spencer would receive a free gift voucher. But as I knelt down on the bathroom floor with a towel, I thought, This is it. I am about to embark on something extraordinary, something profound and, yes, magical, after which I will be *different* somehow, something inside me will have changed for ever.

Of course, the reality was entirely different. I was changed, but not even remotely in the way I had predicted. I'd pored over the stages of labour until I felt I'd almost had a baby, so well acquainted was I with the first and second stages, the 'transition', contractions, dilation, but the distant, neutral language of the books and leaflets carefully omitted the chaos, the mess, the bodily fluids, the loss of control, the loss of power, even. The language of the books assumed that we all had the same labour and produced babies in the same way.

In my mother's day, much of the trauma came from the shock of the unknown – was labour really *like this*? And why had nobody told them? Their husbands had dropped them at the hospital door with their neat little suitcases and off they went with only the vaguest idea of what might happen to them in the subsequent hours. One thing's for sure, though: labouring mothers in those days didn't expect it to be *nice*. The goal was to deliver a healthy baby into the world, not to enrich themselves spiritually in the process. Now, super-prepared, clutching our birth plans in our hands, like eager golden retrievers we bound into the labour ward with the full expectation of a 'great labour': that it will be spiritually empowering, transcendent, even orgasmic, the ecstatic zenith of our lives as women and the fulfillment of our inner beings. And the more we know, the better our labour will be.

My mother faced exactly the same gap between expectation and reality. She had been bustled into hospital fast, before going into labour, because of her pre-eclampsia and high blood pressure, and was examined by Sister, a qualified midwife, when she arrived in the hospital. The other staff, the dreaded student midwives, were barely trained and quivered at the barked orders of Sister: 'Decisions seemed to be passed on by the boss shouting and the trainees quiveringly putting things in the wrong holes,' my mother confided as she described how one unfortunate attempted to fit her womb with a catheter. Mum was mortified: this wasn't the calm, controlled, secure environment she'd been expecting at all. Didn't these people know what they were doing, and where was her doctor?

Nine hours after my waters broke, I was feeling the same grim glimpses of reality. This wasn't the hushed, magical experience I'd imagined either. There was nothing reverential and dignified about being manhandled by my consultant, a loud man in a tweed suit and novelty tie, who groped my stomach a bit, pronounced darkly, 'Not a small baby,' and then retreated into the ether. A visit to the birthing pool had been unedifying, as I sat there under the watchful eye of the midwife in the hot, soupy water, contractions disappearing, turning the colour of a boiled ham. 'This isn't working, is it?' the midwife said.

'No,' I replied glumly, donning my Tweety Bird T-shirt again and making for the bed. (My husband had bought the Tweety Bird T-shirt thinking it was cute and I obliged him by wearing it. It sits now at the bottom of one of the drawers in my wardrobe – every time I open the drawer I get a rush of recognition as it all comes back to me. I have never worn the T-shirt since, but have never thrown it out.) The midwife looked at me disparagingly, as if to say, 'Well, you're just a bit of a failure, aren't you. Can't you simply just get a move on?' In fact, such a failure was I that I was shunted off the labour ward and into a side ward of groaning ladies just like me, who had also 'failed to progress'. We were, to use that term which anyone who has ever had a baby will know and fear, 'Not In Labour'. This expression is used to differentiate between women who are dilating nicely and moving through the system as designed, and those poor sods whose bodies refuse to obey and so they lurk in the shadows of a side ward, moaning gently and fanning themselves with *Hello!* magazine.

*

Mum and I would both endure a period of purgatorial limbo until such time as labour was 'established'. In Mum's case, a hospital doctor then arrived to listen to the baby's movements with a trumpet and informed her that she wasn't 'ready' to have her waters broken to move things along. What is it about hospital staff knowing that you are 'ready'? At this stage, her contractions were coming fast and she was vomiting with each one, 'And could I get anyone to give me a bucket? Eventually some student midwife turned up with one of those kidney-shaped dishes which were useless,' my mother scoffed. She continued to have contractions and to vomit for the next several hours, all the while being assured that of course she wasn't in labour, wondering to herself what on earth this was if it wasn't labour?

In my case, I roamed the corridors of the hospital for the following eighteen hours, clutching a TENS machine to me, which although it had been sold as the very latest in pain relief, its annoying, wasp-like buzzing did not entirely distract me from the pain. The details of my experience are engraved on my memory with a vividness I find remarkable. Unable to remember what happened yesterday, I have no trouble recalling more or less every single moment of this experience eleven years ago with filmic clarity, the shuffles and bumps of the trolleys that rolled along the corridor, the matey shouts of the nursing staff to each other, the sudden gusts of laughter, the stale, overheated air and the clammy discomfort of my clothes, and the occasional rush of activity as the staff would respond to an emergency with shouts and urgency, the loud crash of a trolley as it hit the wall, having been mis-steered around the corner by a midwife on its way to theatre and the curses and admonishments that followed. I remember the confusion about what was happening, or not happening. What had the pregnancy book said, I tried to remember — weren't my contractions supposed to get stronger and more frequent? Why wasn't my body cooperating?

At midnight they told me that my husband would have to go home, what with me being Not In Labour, and then

I began to panic. I had just about been able to cope with the bewilderment if I had the mopper of my brow, utterer of reassurances and bringer of cheese baguettes close by, but now, obeying hospital policy, he was going, and I was about to be left all alone, in pain, trying not to moan too loudly for fear of waking the other mothers-to-be on the ward. I grabbed hold of his wrist and wouldn't let go, muttering in a panicky half-whisper about needing an epidural. My husband tried to utter further 'there, there,' type reassurances, but we were both interrupted by the squeak of nurse's shoe on parquet flooring and the whoosh of the curtain around my bed. An angry-looking midwife, obviously annoyed to have been dragged away from her night-time perusal of *Take a Break*, shuffled over to my bed, held my wrist in a desultory fashion and enquired as to when my husband would be leaving. A series of agitated whispers followed as my husband was urged out of the way and home, and then the midwife laid into me. 'You are *not* in labour, let me tell you. When you are in labour, you will know all about it. The pain will be so bad that you won't be able to speak, so just be quiet and get some rest.' A lengthy lecture followed on the duties of would-be mothers to keep a stiff upper lip, and I felt like a naughty seven-year-old who was moaning about not being able to watch telly after homework.

But she may have had a point. This wasn't labour at all, but a lengthy prequel, which, because of the way my body works, didn't actually get any worse than this wearying,

constant, but just-about-tolerable pain which would ulti-
mately leave me feeling worn out, but would get me to
my destination with the speed of an ancient steam train on
a tour of the scenic bits of Snowdonia – i.e. very slowly
and taking in every stop along the way. And so what –
there's nothing wrong with this, is there? Well, no, but I
find the idea that women are supposed to keep a stiff upper
lip in labour interesting, or that noise is only permitted
when officially 'in labour' and until that designated time a
bit of muffled moaning is all that is permitted.

To ease my distress, I was administered a Temazepam
by a harassed-looking house doctor, which, a smug friend
of mine who had had her child in the middle of a cornfield
or something, assured me was 'absolutely lethal', and not
allowed in Ireland under any circumstances – a bit of a
shame, really. I fell into a welcome hallucinatory slumber,
broken by bizarre David-Lynch-type dreams and that
constant, gut-crunching pain. The same angry midwife
appeared after a few hours to hook the baby up to a
monitor and to assure me once more that I was not in
labour. I couldn't work out whether I was awake or
asleep, in this half-world full of shuffling, moaning and
the occasional howl of distress.

My mother would be given drugs, too, to shut her up,
in her case Pethidine, after which she conked out for a
bit. She came round to the sound of Dad's voice in the
distance, pleading with Sister to allow him to visit her,
even for a moment, to give her the Sunday papers. 'Of

course they said no, and I'll never forget how upset I was. And the next thing, who should be standing beside the bed, only Nana. That was the last straw,' my mother told me bleakly, at which I couldn't suppress a smile – a song-and-dance-routine would hardly have been a useful distraction to my mother in her bewildered state. 'She could only sit there, and I wanted my other half there. And your dad was so anxious, because his own mother had died in childbirth and he wanted to be present.'

So there we were, the lepers of the labour ward, alone, not knowing what the hell was going on, our anxiety and distress having been alleviated not by a reassuring word or two, but by a dose of barbiturates. Mind you, I managed to lose an entirely welcome four hours thanks to my own personal happy pill. When I woke up, at first I didn't know where I was or what on earth I was doing in this place, until I realized that I had actually been asleep. I snaffled half a Snickers bar to distract me from the pain, and lay there for a bit. I hadn't spoken to anyone for several hours and felt somehow bereft. Would I have to have my baby all alone, would anyone ever come and talk to me or would I stay here for ever, in this in-between place? The pain was stronger now, and had been coming in waves for so long that it felt as if it had beaten me altogether. I couldn't fight it any more. Wanting to cry, shout and howl at the same time, I rolled out of bed and managed to shuffle past the midwives' station.

A cheerful Caribbean midwife shouted, 'And where are you off to, my darling?'

'To the bathroom,' I snarled, shuffling off into the distance.

Half an hour later, I had succeeded in filling the bath with two inches of lukewarm water and, crablike, I stepped in, muttering to myself like a crazy woman. Never, ever again would I go through this, I gabbled, all thoughts of the baby now gone; it was all about surviving the moment, until the next moment when I wondered if I would survive that, and so on. I didn't realize that I was now actually in full labour – that 'progression' had happened at last for this abject failure, and that I was entirely alone. I sank back in the water, feeling its modest warmth massaging my back, the icy chill on my stomach, a full ten inches out of the water. I sighed as the waves of pain came, unable to fight them any more . . . and then I drifted off, unbelievably, into a sleep from which a loud snore woke me up. A knock at the door was followed by, 'Are you in there, dear?' The cheerful Caribbean midwife again. I couldn't help laughing to myself, snorting with hysterics and the glee of having 'lost' a half an hour or so. Maybe the next time I woke up, it'd all somehow be over.

*

I was filled with a new purpose. I shuffled out of the bath, into the bloody Tweety Bird T-shirt and marched to the

midwives' station, whose occupants had ignored my dis-
appearance for the last hour or so. 'Would you like a cup
of tea, my dear?' the same cheerful Caribbean midwife
enquired. I drew myself up to my full five foot and
barked, 'No, I would not. I would like an epidural and if
I don't get one, I will kill someone.' I obviously looked
convincing enough because the midwife blanched visibly
and scuttled off through the ward doors. Five minutes
later, a nice midwife, straight out of Oirish central casting
appeared, muttering lots of 'to be sure, to be sure's, and
secured me a doctor's examination.

'Oh,' the pleasant ginger-haired house doctor ex-
claimed, 'you're in labour, eight-and-a-half centimetres.'
You don't bloody say, I thought to myself, as I was
wheeled back to the labour ward, and my husband duly
summoned from his Islington purdah. I had a lovely,
lovely epidural, which allowed me to walk around, and
suddenly I began to chat madly about Simply Red and
football, like some crazed, pain-free lunatic – finally,
there were other human beings with whom to communi-
cate. Lazarus-like, I clutched my drip bag and shuffled
around the room, wittering on in a gay, drug-high
manner.

But then, suddenly, my baby was in some distress, the
heartbeat on the monitor slowing and then speeding up
again. I could hear lots of muttering about meconium and
how the baby would need tests when he came out and
how 'you'll need to push, dear, as we need to get the

baby out quickly'. The epidural, whilst beyond fabulous, having given me renewed energy, had also taken away my ability to work out where I was in the labour and what I should be doing next. So much for control. By now, I was surrounded by slime on my plastic bedding as bits of me leaked and I looked on seemingly outside myself. And what was that loud bellowing sound – who was making all that noise, I wondered? There was no-one else in the room apart from my midwife and bewildered husband. I barely heard her say, 'I'm going to have to cut you, dear. We need to get this baby out. He's getting upset.' At that moment, I couldn't have cared less had she announced that she was going to slit my throat from ear to ear.

And then the baby shot out, as if on a waterslide, expelled from my womb with the force of a missile, caught deftly by the midwife. A large, very cross-looking baby boy was shown to me briefly, sort of waved at me, like an apparition, before being taken away to the little resuscitation table. Under the glare of the lights, he was examined closely and his tiny hands were squeezed for a blood sample to test for infection. 'Give him back,' I moaned, almost to myself, longing to hold him, to examine his tiny, scrunched-up features, his crinkly skin, downy hair and spindly little fingers. I wanted to hold onto him for dear life, to protect him from the noise and bustle of the world which he'd entered. I looked at his body, surprisingly solid on the little resuscitation table, willing them not to cause him too much pain as they squeezed his hands looking for a drop or two of blood. Was this child really mine – had he really come out of *me*? It would seem he had.

I felt a sense of elation, but also a curious sense of vertigo, as all the pushing and pulling, the shrieking and roaring, the pain and the angst was replaced by a blanket of silence. I smiled as the midwife stitched me up, like a roast chicken for the oven, and shouted to her friend out the window that she'd be free for lunch in a few minutes; the baby was weighed and a gust of laughter greeted the fact that he was a full nine pounds; 'And look at the size of you,' the midwife joked. I smiled wanly, not entirely sharing the joke, and clutched my husband's hand. Eventually, having endured his own little Guantanamo, the baby was returned to his parents, seemingly none the worse for wear, and he was placed first in my husband's arms, who cried tears of relief and joy as he examined his son's pink mottled face, fingers cupping his cheeks, a huge yawn revealing a tiny pink tongue, a mewl and a squeak as he wriggled his tiny frame and stretched in the warm air.

*

'We nearly lost you,' my mother's doctor said when she came around, forty-eight hours after giving birth under general anaesthetic. 'I was in a darkened room and my mother was there again,' she remembered, rolling her eyes to heaven, 'and there was no sign of a baby.' The

Master of the hospital appeared by her bedside — an unheard-of event — to murmur reassuring words and to explain that, because of his low birth weight of four pounds eleven ounces, my brother was in an incubator in the ICU. For my mother, this news came at the end of a gruelling forty-eight hours, during which, with her waters broken, the baby became stuck for what seemed like hours. A decision was made to knock her out and to literally pull the baby out, her obstetrician having been summoned by the then-panicky midwife. My mother's protests that she had a cold, which was obvious to all because of the hacking cough that had accompanied her labour, were ignored. Knowing that the baby was unwell, 'The registrar appeared and asked me what I was going to call the child,' Mum told me. 'My mother said, "Oh, she hasn't made any decision yet," and I rose up from my bed and said, "Ian Denis".' It was as if, even in this small matter, my mother was trying to make herself heard.

For my mother, the trauma of her first labour and delivery has marked her, filled her with a rage which persists to this day, a host of unanswered questions and a feeling of powerlessness that I recognize because I have felt it too.

A full ten years after giving birth to my son, I can truly say that this was the worst experience of my entire life, and the best. The reality fell so far short of my expectations, of the mystical, empowering experience that I would have simply because I had prepared for it so diligently. For a long time, if people asked me what my birth experience had been like, I would rant and rave, and yet, could it have been any other way? Perhaps the London midwives were right simply to let nature take its course, even if that was very, *very* slowly. Should I have been left in a bath by myself for an hour without anyone checking on me? Possibly not, but then the staff in busy teaching hospitals are, well, busy, and that's the key – too busy to offer women the support and reassurance they need. Perhaps if I had just had a nice midwife close by, who was able to monitor my progress with me and to keep a closer eye on the situation, she might not have allowed it to get to distress-level; I might not have needed an epidural and an episiotomy and he wouldn't have needed to have his hands gouged to test for blood infections. Who knows? But for me, hospital was where it had all started to go wrong.

When I was having my first child, I never thought twice about having him in hospital. I met other mothers at the antenatal clinics who had ordered their birthing pools and joked about reinforcing the kitchen floor to take the weight of the water and I marvelled at their courage, whilst silently congratulating myself on having taken the 'safest' option, just like Mum, sensible woman that I was. At the time, I felt that it was a fairly straightforward choice between safety and danger, between science, which I trusted, and nature, that most unreliable of forces. Now, I am altogether less sure.

My mother had trusted her carefully chosen obstetrician implicitly, thankful for the developments that allowed her to avail of his superior skills. Twenty years before, she would have had to make do with an overworked midwife, or, as did most country women, a 'handy-woman', doctors being scarce and prohibitively expensive. Often a local woman with no formal training, this handy-woman would have been handed the job by her own mother and would have gained experience simply by attending birth after birth. Kevin Kearn's *Dublin Tenement Life* refers to Ma Lakey, who would come in and supervise the birth, the bed having been laid with newspaper and the hot water ready. Her job then was to hold the mother down whilst she had the baby (she also delivered the placenta, crucial at the time before drugs, to avoid infection), to tidy up the whole house and to come in every single day for nine days afterwards to take care of the new mother for the princely sum of half a crown.[5]

According to the sociologist Caitriona Clear, the midwife on Tory Island owed her popularity to her ability to recite decades of the Rosary whilst the mother-to-be was in labour.[6] Indeed, up until the 1950s in Ireland, even the Masters of the maternity hospitals were unconvinced that hospital was best, it being a breeding ground, if you'll

5. *Dublin Tenement Life, An Oral History*, Kevin Kearns, Gill & Macmillan, Dublin, 1994. Quoted in *Women of the House: Women's Household Work in Ireland, 1922–1961*, Caitriona Clear, IAP, Dublin, 2000.

6. Ibid. p. 107.

excuse the pun, for germs and infection. And doctors then didn't have the experience in obstetrics that they do now. Dr Michael Solomons, a student doctor in the 1940s in Dublin, is quoted by Caitriona Clear as saying: 'While in our amateurish way we would try to assess how a birth was progressing, the opinion of an experienced mother, or of her friends, would prove far more dependable than our own.'

But by the time my mother had Ian, 'The doctor was God,' as she told me, and hers was, according to those in the know, one of the best in the country. And yet, her experience – for a variety of reasons – was a nightmare trauma from beginning to end.

Now, I am not suggesting that problems arose due to the hospitalization of my mother's labour or her choice of a doctor to supervise it – after all, the midwife had been in charge for a large part of it – and there could have been any number of reasons for the difficulties, but a certain pattern emerges: the handing over by the midwife of her instincts and power to a doctor, the pervasive feeling that a mother in labour was an impediment to the smooth progress of things, and the phenomenon of Maternal Deafness. After much discussion with my fellow mothers, a consensus arose that some problems which occurred in childbirth had to do with them simply not being listened to. 'I tried to tell the doctor/midwife/student-midwife in semi-hysterics because it was my first birth, but she wouldn't listen,' is a refrain I have heard more than once.

In my own first labour, as I sat or stood, moaned or
remained silent, I got the distinct impression that the
medical staff thought I was a pain in the ass basically, an
eejit who knew nothing whatsoever about the experience
she was having and couldn't be relied upon to follow her
own instincts about what felt right or wrong. Wouldn't it
be simpler, I could almost hear them say, if they could
dispose of us annoying birthing women altogether? And
that the answers to difficulties may not *always* be medical,
that it isn't just a case of whipping out the vacuum cleaner
if a baby doesn't make an appearance instantly, whereupon
an episiotomy follows as sure as night follows day.

I have since had two babies, quite happily, on the
lovely Community Midwives scheme in Ireland. Here, a
dedicated team of midwives care for women throughout
their pregnancy, labour and afterwards, visiting the new
mother at home. I opted to go into hospital for the births,
followed by an 'early release' six hours after the birth,
and the experience could not have been more different. I
still opted for the hospital – old habits die hard, after all
– but for me, the argument is not actually about home
vs. hospital, doctor vs. midwife, Maya chanting vs. elec-
tive Caesarean, but about having some say in the births of
my own babies, having someone listen to me properly
and trust that I know what I'm talking about, rather than
telling me what's happening, what with it being my labour
and all, and letting me get on with it. When I had my
daughter and then my youngest son, there was no noise

or bustle, just a quiet room with the midwife, a copy of *Hello!* magazine to pore over and some pleasant conversation to pass the time – no monitors, no beeping and whirring and clicking, and no pain relief. Before you admire my Amazonian strength, this isn't to say that I didn't *want* it – for the birth of my third child, I remember feeling distinctly weary at the thought of another bloody natural labour – but I didn't actually need it. With support, encouragement and peace and quiet, and with the understanding that they would follow my lead, I was able to produce my beautiful daughter and my gorgeous terrier-like son with only a modicum of fuss, with a quicker physical recovery and with happier memories of my birth experience.

Take It from Me

* Accept the fact that no mother in her right mind will tell you the truth about childbirth, give you the heads-up about the sheer ghastly hell of it all, because if they did, you would run screaming, or refuse to have the baby unless totally unconscious or at least on some hallucinogen. Childbirth remains a mystery to those who have not gone through it for a very good reason.

* Follow your own instincts about what you think you want when you have your baby – if that is bringing

your own yurt into the labour ward, fine, or hiking up the Amazon to find the world's most wizened midwife to supervise the birth, or alternatively hiring some shit-hot obstetrician, that's also just fine. And don't let anyone else tell you otherwise. Becoming a mother means that you, personally, become a receptacle for a lifetime's unsolicited advice so it's best to begin to ignore it all now. No one knows better than you what you need.

* You will, of course, have ideas on how you would like the birth of your baby to be, if I haven't succeeded in totally putting you off in this chapter, and you need to write them down and press them into the medic's hand. As they suffer from professional deafness when it comes to mothers to be, you will need to let them know what you want. However, it's probably best to be realistic. I had friends who have endured labours from hell because they felt that to take an epidural was somehow failing, when the midwife was actually begging them to have it; if you are reasonably flexible, you won't be too devastated when things don't go according to plan. Again, it's not a competition to see which of us can have the 'best' birth.

* Bring every little home comfort into the hospital with you: a year's supply of egg-and-cress sandwiches,

which should make the process a bit gaseous, but there we are; a king-size Snickers bar, plenty of liquid, and several pairs of comfy pyjamas. Other items are more essential, if a little daunting: I couldn't get over the idea of paper knickers before I went into hospital but they are needed, as is an airline neck cushion upon which to rest your sore bottom. I actually brought a novel with me, the thought of which makes me fairly snort with laughter now – how I thought I would have the time for a little light reading is beyond me. I did have a nice chat with one of the doctors about the book. He had read it though. Ten years later, I have never finished it.

* If you have had a traumatic birth experience, talk to other mothers about it. It's tempting to bury it, to try to forget it, but the emotional impact of it can be overwhelming and other mothers will listen, swap stories and howl along with you. To discover that others' birth experiences were just as shattering as yours is hugely comforting.

Chapter Three

A 'Natural' Mother

'Unless regular hours and strict punctuality are enforced, the baby cannot be well trained and most people will agree that, apart from his physical well-being, which must also suffer, a badly trained baby is a nuisance to himself and to all those with whom he comes into contact.'

Nurse Margaret Laine, 1931,
www.todaysparent.com

'Are you as fussy about clean hair, clean nails, becoming clothes, well-fitting shoes as you were two years ago? Maternity is no excuse for sloppiness, but rather an incentive to a more attractive personality.'

Canadian broadcaster Kate Aitken, 1955,
in Ann Douglas, *You'll Spoil that Child!:
Vintage Mother and Baby Advice*[7]

7. Source: www.squidoo.com/lensmasters/anndouglas

One of the most insidious of the myths of motherhood is that we are all destined to take to it 'naturally' – that it is somehow within us as women, part of our genetic make-up; that once our babies are born, we instinctively 'know' how to mother them, recalling instincts from the primeval swamp to feed, clothe and care for our new-borns, and if we don't possess this bit of DNA, if we don't connect with our babies immediately, or flail around uncertainly with nappies, vests, bathing and feeding, we feel that we are somehow failures. And the contradictory myth, that we spoilt twenty-first-century women are unable to mother 'naturally', as did the generations before us, is even more powerful; that, used to having things our own way for at least the first thirty years of our lives, we struggle to accept the limitations on our self-fulfillment that having a baby imposes.

I have felt that the selfish-mother myth is precisely that – a stick with which to beat contemporary mothers, to make us feel that we are less than we should be. And yet, when I talked to my mother about the early days of mothering, expecting her to nod her head in agreement at the picture I painted of a demented, frazzled mother struggling to accept the changes in her life, she looked at me blankly. I prodded a bit: surely she must have found it hard going, after all she'd been through? But no, the picture she painted was of a woman who enjoyed the babyhood of her children wholeheartedly and, whilst she might have worried from time to time, she doesn't seem to have subjected the whole thing to the same kind of paralysing self-scrutiny as her daughter. Motherhood does indeed appear to have come to my mother 'naturally', in spite of the unpromising beginning to her son's life. She was a willing and enthusiastic mother who accepted who she was and where this next step in her life had taken her.

*

Nonetheless, Mum's first encounter with her newborn was inauspicious: 'Your brother looked like a baby from Calcutta, all wizened and scrawny,' was her politically incorrect description of my brother. (In those days, due to the popularity of Mother Theresa, all Irish people associated Calcutta with grinding poverty and malnourished children.) She found it hard to disguise her shock at this little old man-baby, with his tiny shrunken features, so unlike my strapping twenty-first-century baby, almost twice the size of his uncle at birth, a warm and wobbly coating of fat already covering his ample frame. I was on a high as I was wheeled back to the baby ward, like Harold Abrahams in *Chariots of Fire*, flying on a cloud of elation, gabbling away like a woman possessed, clutching my son to me tightly in his dayglo orange babygro – the only one that would fit him. His puffy features were pink with exertion and fatigue and covered in tiny scratches following his two-day fight to get out into the world. He looked more robust than all of the other babies on the ward, the tiny five-pounders born to young Islington mums, who all gathered around my bed exclaiming, 'Ooh, innee big?'

This tiny person was so totally 'here', examining the ridiculous 'scratch mittens' that I had placed on his hands, inky blue eyes staring up at me, ears cocked for all of the interesting noises going on around him. As a newborn, he was already fully formed, which came as a shock. I hadn't realized that babies were real people – developing, but very much themselves. This little man who, until an hour ago had been wriggling around inside me, my little passenger, was now separate from me – was now out in the world, his own self, lying on his back, nose in the air, looking for all the world like the Pope in state, arms flailing in his sleep as he dreamed.

I looked around the twenty-four-bedded Princess Margaret Ward, a sickly-green-painted overheated room occupied by cheerful mums and their tiny little bundles, swathed in elaborate matinée jackets and matching bonnets, and wondered if they, too, were feeling it, this sense of wonder mixed with an anxiety about exactly what it was they were expected to *do* with this tiny person. They all seemed to be so confident, I thought, shifting their babies from arm to arm, wiping their tiny bottoms and flicking through magazines whilst they slept. I looked at my son as he gave a gusty sigh in the plastic bassinet that had been pulled up to my bed, afraid to move in case he woke up. I thought – What do I do now?

*

Initially, exhausted by the birth and the Temazepam/ epidural cocktail that he had unknowingly ingested, he slept . . . and slept . . . and slept. I looked at him in wonder as he shuffled and snuffled and jumped in fright as his arms jolted back in his sleep. How perfect, I thought, gazing at him adoringly, watching his eyes flicker in sleep and listening to the little squeaks that he emitted. 'Try to get some sleep,' the nurse told me kindly, when she came to check on us. *Sleep*, I thought to myself, sure what would I want with that? I was crazed with excitement and couldn't shut my brain off for a moment – this was the best day of my life, I had a real, live baby asleep beside me, wasn't it fantastic . . . on and on my brain spun whilst the hours passed and my son slept. Darkness fell and a hush descended on the ward as mothers and babies snuggled down for the night. I lay there, mind racing, thoughts flickering to the past few hours and days, the events of which played over and over in my mind. I tried to close my eyes, but my son would wriggle and squirm in his sleep and my eyes would flick open again. Did he need me, was he too hot or cold? Did his nappy need changing and if so, how would I do it? I hadn't changed a nappy since my sister's twenty-six years before and I had stuck the safety pin of the cloth nappy into her leg in the process. Should I be worried about him sleeping, should I wake him up for a feed? What did the book say about frequency of feeding?

And then, as the clock struck twelve that night, he awoke, his tiny face contorted with pain and rage, and he let out a roar that would fell timber. He roared and roared, that ululating, hysterically panicky cry that mothers of newborns will recognize – Do Something *Now*. I picked him up and held him tight, whereupon he roared more. I jiggled and jounced, shushed and there-there-d, but his cries became more frantic. I sat on my bed and attempted to feed him, desperately trying to remember Brenda's memo on breastfeeding from the antenatal classes: did I clasp him to my bosom or hold him away slightly, did I tilt his head back or push his chin down? Oh, help, I thought. His cries became shrieks of panic and so I stuffed him onto the breast, whereupon he took great, desperate gulps of milk, like a parched traveller who has discovered an oasis in the Sahara. Silence reigned for a few moments, and I could feel the others in the ward sigh with relief. But after a few minutes, he tore himself away and began to roar again, contorted with wind from having scarfed his dinner with such enthusiasm.

I popped him onto my shoulder, patting him frantically and singing tunelessly. Maybe there was something seriously wrong with him, I began to think, panic rising.

My son's night-time bellowing sessions attracted the unwelcome attention of the night nurse, a truly fearsome forty-stone Eastern European lady with size-eleven flat feet, one of the dreaded 'agency' midwives who would replace the lovely day staff, who all seemed to simmer with an inner rage at life's unfairness and sought to alleviate it by drinking copious amounts of tea and reading celebrity magazines. They did not want to be disturbed under any circumstances and certainly not by anything as annoying as a crying baby.

This particular exemplar of the profession stalked past my bed, the soles of her shoes slapping against the lino, muttering about 'scriming babeez'. She pulled back the curtain surrounding the bed and fixed me with a glare, before extending her hands to me. Meekly, I handed over my son to her, suppressing the urge to wail as loudly as he. She flung him onto her shoulder and proceeded to bang him robustly on the back to 'vind' him, thereby making him 'scrim' even more. She banged him on the back another few times, his wails competing with the loud slapping of her hand on his back. Finally, with a sigh of disappointment, she handed him back to me, my own little time bomb to diffuse. I looked at him anxiously, his mouth wide open, tonsils vibrating with the force of his crying.

'Show me,' she pointed to my T-shirt.

'Show you what?' I yelled over the din, unable to think what she meant. I looked down at my T-shirt as if it would give me a sign. Magda the Terrible pointed at my chest area and repeated, 'Show me.' Tentatively, I lifted my T-shirt. Perhaps she wanted to correct my son's position on the breast so that he'd feed more easily? Magda sighed gustily and leaned in over my still-wailing baby, grabbing one of my breasts as if it were an icing bag needing to be squeezed. 'Tsk . . . you'll never feed a baby with breasts like that. Breasts no good,' she uttered gnomically. Breasts like *what?* I wondered, what was wrong with them? I examined the icing bags for evidence of any malfunction – what was I doing to him with my killer breasts – would he be better off with a nice bottle of Cow & Gate like some of the other mums were giving theirs, not wrestling with my attempts to stuff my malfunctioning appendage in his sleepy mouth? Magda the Terrible said nothing further but simply slapped her way back across the ward to her station, muttering under her breath, leaving me stunned, worried and with a still-screaming baby.

The pattern continued for the next forty-eight hours in Hades with my son sleeping soundly all day and roaring all night, much to the annoyance of my fellow inmates, as it would set theirs off and a cacophony of wailing would ensue, like some mournful pandemic sweeping the ward. In spite of my defective breasts, my son seemed to be getting some sort of food, glugging away in the early hours, but Magda's words rang in my ear in constant reproach. Was he getting the right kind of food or would he succumb to early starvation? Why was I this demented banshee and not a smiling beatific person who would understand and respond to her son's every unspoken need? Whatever happened to Caroline Ingalls? Why wasn't I a 'natural' at this job – isn't that what real mothers were?

Even when I plucked up the courage to change him, it was All Wrong. I had gingerly pulled the nappy off his tiny little bottom, marvelling at how flat and red it was and wondering why it was glued to the nappy by what looked like tar. I racked my brains to remember what this alarming-looking substance could be – was he seriously ill? Should I be worried? 'It's just meconium,' a passing nurse assured me, 'nothing to worry about.' Emboldened, I gathered together my changing mat and wipes, and proceeded to try to unstick some of the tar from his red buttocks. After a few deft strokes with the wipes, there was only a small bit of black chewing gum adhering to his bottom. A job well done, I congratulated myself. Perhaps I was getting the hang of it all at last. I sighed with relief and reached over to fetch another wipe out of the pink packet when I was distracted by a shriek of alarm and turned my head to see what the commotion was. An angry midwife was standing over me. 'What on *earth* are you doing?' she bellowed.

I looked at her blankly. Wasn't it obvious?

'Don't you know that you don't use wipes on a newborn,' she hollered. 'You'll burn the bottom off him.' She fixed me with a glare and strode off, leaving me quaking and on the verge of tears. Had I rubbed his little bottom raw, I thought frantically, and what were wipes for, if they weren't for wiping? A few moments later, she returned with a cardboard bowl filled with water and a wad of cotton wool. 'This is what you use,' she barked, before marching off again. I sniffed furiously and dabbed a bit more, before putting on a fresh nappy and hugging him to me tightly, his mouth next to my ear. He made little mewing noises and gurgled a bit, wriggling his legs in relief at having a nice fresh bottom even if it had been sandpapered by his mother. I murmured and sang to him, crying all the time.

*

My mother endured a similarly bleak few days in hospital following Ian's birth. She would queue with all of the other mothers, lined up like soldiers at the end of their beds for the daily bath the hospital insisted on, in the single bathroom at the end of the ward. 'We had to line up and stay in line until bathtime,' she remembered. One day, she watched in horror as another mother keeled over in a dead faint and started bleeding all over the floor: 'After that, I told the nurses that I wasn't a dirty person and that I'd wash myself,' was my mother's terrified response. The regime at the hospital was unforgiving – unlike another city maternity hospital where parties were held at visiting time and a general air of jollity prevailed, in this place, merriment of any sort was frowned upon, as was the encouragement of mother-and-baby bonding that we take for granted and which helps us to establish breastfeeding, amongst other things. Some mothers did have their babies with them during the day but all babies were whipped away to the nursery at night to get their 'rest', being presented to nursing mothers only when they woke, and only at scheduled times. Mothers were strictly forbidden from entering the nursery.[8] As my siblings and I were all tiny babies and thus in the nursery at all times, my mother quickly gave up on the idea of breastfeeding.

Of course, there is something essentially incompatible about healthy babies with different needs and hospital, but

8. In Ireland, there is a certain ambivalence about breastfeeding: in her essay 'Infant Feeding' in Patricia Kennedy's *Motherhood in Ireland* (Mercier Press, 2004), Maureen Dillon Hurney explains that in 1951 in the National Maternity Hospital, 51 per cent of mothers breastfed their babies. By 1982, the figure had declined to 32 per cent, and never exceeded 33 per cent throughout the 1990s. There are a number of reasons for this, but Hurney points the finger at rigid hospital schedules, the offering of supplementary feeds and test-weighing for weight gain as contributory factors. Nowadays, of course, breastfeeding is encouraged in hospital, and babies are with their mothers at all time, but stories abound of harried staff being too busy to help mothers with breastfeeding or, too eagerly acquiesing to requests from struggling mothers for a bottle.

my mother's experience made me wonder if 'natural' is in fact something we do better nowadays, where babies are close to their mother at all times in hospital, where midwives will at least try to help with breastfeeding and where the regime is more relaxed. Maybe I'm being too hard on myself as a panicky first-timer – no, didn't know not to use wipes, but my instincts, to keep my baby dry, warm and fed, were very much there. But the spoilt brat part of the myth is definitely nearer the mark. Even though my mother was unsure of herself and Ian initially failed to thrive, she didn't panic: younger and more flexible than I, she didn't expect to control the universe and thus wasn't felled by this tiny scrap of humanity. The problem for me was not actually that I didn't know what I was doing, although I didn't, but that I simply didn't trust myself to learn with my baby. I assumed that I would 'know it all', and that any gaps could be filled in from a variety of parenting books and my own innate knowledge of what was right for my baby. I felt that mothering could be learned as a series of techniques in the same way as Spanish, or computers: my instinct and my knowledge of my own baby simply wouldn't do. My learning curve, to use that horrible expression, would be steep, and would have rather less do to with acquiring knowledge than with listening to myself, something that my mother, in the Dark Ages, was able to do.

*

After three days in hospital my mother was released on
5 December, but would not be joined by her baby until
Christmas Eve 1963, when a telegram arrived informing
her that her son was now ready to go home, a typically
impersonal touch which Mum considered the final indignity in her dealings with the hospital. 'I mean, could they
not have telephoned,' she asked me, cheeks flushed with
anger, as if the insult had happened only yesterday. 'We
had to rush to the chemist for formula and last-minute
things, and the house was full of visitors – it was like a
hotel.' My father's family were visiting from England, my
father's elderly grandfather was still resident in the house
and inviting all of his cronies in at all hours of the day and
night, and Nana and Jack arrived from Granddad's latest
posting in Sligo, settling themselves down on the sofa to
watch slides of Mum and Dad's honeymoon in Austria.
When my mother returned home in triumph, Nana was
there to bounce the baby up and down and to offer plenty
of daft and unwanted advice. And even though she had
faint collywobbles about 'being responsible for this tiny
screaming thing, this life', she would appear to have got
on with it happily. She consulted Dr Spock's book and
followed his advice about getting Ian into a routine, with
plenty of sleep in a darkened room and nice walks in the
fresh air, when she would wheel our giant pram up to
her friend Betty, whose pregnancy kept her bedridden, or
to her beloved uncle Sean, Nana's younger brother, who

lived a nice stroll away. The quiet, calm routine needed by 'Baby' was established.

When I got home to the safety of my little first-floor flat, my son crumpled into his car seat, looking for all the world like Yoda, with his crinkly face and slightly hairy ears, I was accompanied by my watchful husband, the receptacle for much of my angst over previous days and who was carefully circling around his wife and child, unsure of his position in the new household, not that, frankly, I gave a rat's ass, unfair though this clearly was. I had eyes only for the baby and for striving to be the best mother I could be, and this was a full-time job. My poor husband, who had so nobly supported me in my pregnancy and birth, was on his own, which would, in time, bring its own problems.

But initially, the 'high' of the early days carried me through. I was so relieved to be out of hospital and was nicely distracted from the realities of motherhood by my very own hordes of visitors: my parents, my English relatives, my husband's family; the teacups rattled and the champagne flowed as they marvelled at the baby's size, eyeing my small frame with amusement (which was not shared by me) and busying themselves with trips to mystifying places on the furthest reaches of the M4 with exotically un-Irish names like Lakeside Thurrock in search of baby essentials. I smiled and nodded and agreed that the baby was simply huge, all the while feeling slightly outside of myself. I tried to ignore the nagging voices in my head telling me that I wasn't doing it right: that I wasn't feeding him properly, that, in spite of all of the evidence to the contrary, I wasn't a 'proper' mother.

And when they all left, all of the emotions I had put on hold overcame me. I simply was not prepared for the tidal wave coming towards me of unexpected and alarming anger, frustration and of buried feelings and memories now popping to the surface, of a general feeling of complete helplessness and doubts about how I might forge a relationship with a new person, all of which would alter me completely. This rollercoaster was exhilarating, joyous and amazing, a truly life-changing event, but it was also bewildering, mystifying and exhausting.

*

My first hurdle was breastfeeding, the successful mastery of which provoked in me a kind of hysteria. The feeling that you alone are responsible for your baby's growth, whether you breast or bottle-feed him/her, is elating and daunting at the same time, and it is here that the myth of 'natural' mothering falls apart: much as we might enthuse about the benefits of breastfeeding, the simple fact of the matter is it's a bitch to get the hang of. I have no idea why some feminists refer to breastfeeding as being orgasmic, involving as it does several weeks of excruciating discomfort as the skill is learnt, the horror of cracked nipples, the application of many foul-smelling unguents to said nipples, the purchasing of breast pads to place in the greying maternity bra (they are always greying, even if they are brand new, to leave us in no doubt as to their resolute unsexiness), the astonishment of watching one's breasts swell to rock-hard proportions, or, horrors, leak. It seems that they take on a life of their own, filling with milk at the baby's slightest cry, at the fish counter in the supermarket, or at the opening credits to *EastEnders*, leaking unexpectedly, leaving the front of your T-shirt chilly with soggy milk. Whatever happened to those pert little 32-Ds that filled that bikini on Ibiza – how did they transform into these udders, barely contained by the harness purchased in the maternity section of Arnott's department store? Why do cabbage leaves have an entirely new use? Why do we endure the pain and fever of mastitis in order to persevere with this entirely 'natural' activity?

Again, 'natural' is the key here. When I started breast-feeding, I made the fatal error of assuming that because it was natural, it was therefore easy. But it's not. It's a faintly bewildering process in which, interestingly, your baby is not much wiser than you, like learning some fiend-ishly difficult Argentinean tango in which there is a lot of tripping up and falling over oneself before finally the steps are learned. The experts refer to 'learned instinct' when they talk about breastfeeding, and they are right. Both you and the baby instinctively know that breastfeeding is, well, *there*, but you both have to learn to get it right.

I still remember the agonies of attempting to breastfeed

my son whilst following the draconian 'advice' of two breastfeeding gurus in a fearsome pink manual with a title like *Breast or Death* (I exaggerate). These two women believed in constant feeding and 'wearing' of baby to encourage a bond, offering the breast when the baby so much as farted and not allowing my little bundle out of my arms for a single moment in case he might, at some unspecified time, when I might be further than five feet away, need the breast. Diagrams told me of the 'correct' position for feeding and warned me of various perils, all of which would be entirely my fault, of course. Needless to say, my slavish following of their advice nearly drove me to nervous exhaustion as I examined diagrams, turning the book, or myself, upside down to get a better look, and to get my son to open his mouth to 'latch on', with the ensuing pain which would literally make my toes curl. Early breastfeeding became an endurance test, with me steeling myself for the initial alarming dart of agony, which would then subside to a painful but persistent throbbing as the feed progressed and would leave me blinking to see the television through tears of discomfort.

And of course the dragons in *Breast or Death* failed to mention that breastfed babies wake more often, because they drink the milk differently to bottle-fed babies, tending to snack a bit more and return to the source more often, rather than filling their tummies with thick milk and dozing away for the rest of the afternoon. And that, when baby is having a growth spurt, or when you are tired at night, sometimes supply will not meet demand, leaving you feeling like a wrung-out dishcloth and baby eyeing you beadily, hungry for more. I am not ashamed to say that, after a few days of this carry-on with my son, I dispatched my husband to the supermarket at three o'clock in the morning to purchase a bottle and formula. Junior proceeded to guzzle down four ounces of formula after breastfeeding all night which, whilst it gave me a much needed break from the cycle and ensured a reasonable night's sleep, of course caused me to start worrying about not having enough milk for him and that he might permanently be starving, not to mention having committed the cardinal sin of 'topping up' his feeds with formula, from which God knows what other sins might follow.

After three weeks, I had a moment where I felt I simply couldn't go on, the discomfort seeming to be too much for a bit. I had horrible mastitis, which had given me flu-like symptoms and a lot of pain. I finally gave in and went to the doctor, who promptly started me on an antibiotic. I shuffled back home, exhausted and in agony, and swallowed two antibiotic tablets, as prescribed. A few moments later, I threw them up again in the bathroom, and, hunched over the toilet bowl, I wept great, gulping sobs of self pity.

*

Even though her own baby wasn't thriving as he should be, Mum didn't start to beat herself up about it: 'I did feel very much afraid because Ian was very thin and cried a lot, and he was very slow to thrive,' so she consulted a local paediatrician, a mother like herself, who brightly said, 'We'll fatten him up,' and provided Mum with lots of advice about feeding schedules, 'and by the summer he'd caught up with other babies'. And that was that, no hand-wringing or second-guessing. On the other hand, here was I with a healthy baby, in a state because I was failing to live up to the notion of perfection I had blithely envisaged.

For me, it wasn't going according to plan – the information leaflets in the health centre had tasteful pictures of joyous mother and baby duos feeding cheerfully on them, not wailing babies and mothers with hair standing on end. And my son was a restless, colicky baby, who never slept for more than an hour or so at a time. The lack of sleep nearly drove me demented and left me a cranky, depressed shadow of my former self. And, if I'm honest because, unlike Mum with her lovely routines, I didn't want to give in to the way my life had changed, to alter *my* nice routines – to sleep in the afternoon with him instead of walking around Islington, him asleep in his sling, me hallucinating with fatigue as I tramped up Upper Street. Eventually, having become quite frankly depressed, muttering to myself and developing an obsession with *Trauma: Life in the ER*, in which a variety of North Americans were wheeled into hospital emergency rooms with GSWs (that's gunshot wounds to the uninitiated) or other injuries – on at the handy time of 1 a.m. – I resigned myself to the fact that I would simply have to sleep. And so, I would curl up with him under a blanket on the bed in the afternoon, and awake an hour or so later, refreshed enough to make the dinner. The days became little bursts of activity, broken by oases of sleep from which my son and I would emerge like bushbabies, woken by the tinny *Match of the Day* soundtrack of the ice-cream van outside.

*

It would seem that even though I wanted to be the best mother that I could, I simply couldn't let go of the woman I used to be, at least not without a fight, or without the kind of simmering resentment that would barely have crossed my mother's mind. I was still consumed by the breastfeeding and the self-doubt and the fact that my son wasn't the smiling, obedient, *easy* baby I'd been expecting. I had thought that babies were a generic brand and all did more or less the same things – but of course babies are people, each with their own personality. My son's was lovely, gentle and mild, but he was plagued by colic and reflux. I would diligently feed him, whereupon he would throw up and cry for the next hour or so, legs drawn up in pain, mouth wide open, howling. It was as if I had given him poison, something that made him ill, not milk. Of course, logically I knew that he simply had colic, which wasn't helped by the fact that he was hungry and tucked away more milk than he probably needed. But emotionally, I wondered if the stresses of my life before I had him made him this uneasy, restless and fretful, his bumpy sojourn in my tummy marked by anxiety, job loss and general gloom. I came to the conclusion that it was all my fault, that he didn't like me basically, because I was an inferior mother, a bad model, and should ideally be exchanged for a much better one.

*

I didn't realize at the time that I did have a bond with my son, even though it wasn't the idealized one I had expected. I held him constantly, in awe of his perfection as a human being, loving his snuffling and shuffling in his cot, his tiny arms thrown into the air, the way he would fold up like a little piece of origami in his baby seat, Wee Willie Winkie hat on his head, chin resting on his tummy as he snoozed away; the way his eyes would watch the television screen avidly as he watched the European Cup with his dad, propped up in a beanbag. I protected him diligently, ensuring that he was warm and comfortable and fed until his little eyes drooped with fullness. But at the same time, I would look at him and think . . . nothing really. I was simply too exhausted to feel the kind of emotions I thought I should be feeling – maternal love, a rosy glow, a happy wonderment, and occasionally, when he would projectile vomit and poo at the same time, soaking another babygro, or refuse to sleep for more than forty minutes at a time, I might think, 'I don't really like you.' Breasts leaking, demented from lack of sleep, filthy from being unable to shower in case he would scream and I might not immediately be able to snap to attention and respond to his every need, surrounded by nappies and babygros in various states of cleanliness – I slipped into depression.

Unlike my peers, who seemed to trundle through the days relatively happily with their little bundles, I fell apart. Every night, when he would wake every hour on the hour, feeding fretfully and refusing to settle, I would think dark thoughts and sometimes feel an anger towards him so powerful that it would terrify me. I hasten to say that it went no further than nightmarish thoughts – I never acted on it, or even came close to it, although once or twice I had to leave the room to get away from the constant crying and sit in front of *This Morning* for a few moments to calm the ringing in my ears, to quell the urge to flee, or to break something, or both.

The other emotion I experienced was a deep sense of shame, that I was the only mum not coping, the only person in the world who was a terrible mother, who thought dark thoughts in the wee hours and hated herself for it. And nothing anyone said made any difference to me. 'You're doing fine,' the midwives reassured me, impressed by my son's weight gain and bonny appearance, by his clean nappies and babygros, but I knew that I was only faking it and that, deep down, I was a huge failure.

When my son was three weeks old, my husband went back to work. How he was able to get out the door is a mystery, as I was practically hanging off of his ankles, begging him not to leave me alone with the baby. It seemed that this tiny person was so much 'bigger' than me – his needs too overwhelming for me to meet, and too relentless for me to respond to as I felt a proper mother should. Every wail and squeak seemed like a personal reproach – 'I need something and you are not giving it to me.' I am ashamed to say that I wept and wailed, begged and cajoled to no avail: my bewildered husband had already taken too much time off work and had to return.

I was hysterical and panicky and the walls seemed to be closing in on me. In a panic, I rang my local GP surgery and it was politely suggested that I come to visit their counsellor. I sat and sobbed in a chair covered in ethnic cushions, baby strapped to my front in a sling; I poured it all out: my fear of my baby's needs and not being able to meet them, my sense of failure, to which she nodded sympathetically. Finally, during a lull, she asked 'Would you like him to go away?'

All of the wittering and the wailing and weeping dropped away. I stopped dead in my tracks. This woman had recognized that behind all the guff, there was something else going on. I was now being asked to tell the truth and not to hide behind a litany of anxious moaning. I nodded tearfully.

I was not taken away in handcuffs, nor were Social Services called because I had told this woman that I wanted my baby to go away. She and I both knew that I didn't – but what I did want to 'go away' was the responsibility of motherhood and the constant needs of my son. People talk about moments of epiphany and here, in the sick-painted environs of the doctor's surgery, was mine. It was as if a pair of existential fingers had been snapped and I suddenly 'got' it. My son was mine and I loved him and no, he wasn't going to 'go away' and so I needed to rise to the occasion somehow, to get on with it and to deal with the fact that it was difficult, but worthwhile.

*

Looking back, I realize that to eulogize my mother's era as the fount of something wholesomely natural is misleading. Mum had other, poignant reasons for having enjoyed the baby stage as much as she did. 'I liked the baby stage', she told me, 'because having a two-year-old in the house for twenty years put you off the older stage,' referring to the tantrums and unpredictable behaviour that went with my brother's autism, which persisted until his teens. But even so, she was a relaxed and happy mother to all of her babies, a real 'natural'. Part of the reason I struggled was because I felt that, unlike her, I was not a 'natural' mother. When I had my son, others said, 'Oh, dear, you really did struggle, didn't you? It didn't come *naturally*, did it?' Failure to be a 'natural' mother was, it seemed, a crime. But which of us can claim to be a 'natural' with our babies? The process of learning about them must be the same for each of us, no matter how quickly we bond with them, but with the constant perfection and fulfilment of motherhood being shoved down our throats, it can be hard to accept when it all doesn't go according to plan.

On one of her lovely reassuring visits, Hilda the Health Visitor sat on my sofa munching fruit shortcake biscuits and sagely said, 'It's so hard for you women nowadays, isn't it?', which left me vaguely bewildered. What did she mean? How could it be any harder for mothers nowadays, when we had 'so much': husbands who are expected to share the burden, money to spend on the best for our babies, excellent maternity care? I overcame my maternity wobbles precisely because I had such a lot of good support.

Much later, I understood what she meant. We have such high expectations of motherhood nowadays: now that it is no longer an inevitability, but a choice, we freight it with so much expectation when it comes along: that it will be the sum total of our fulfilment as human beings. How often have we opened a glossy magazine and had some well-known mother proclaim mistily that 'motherhood has changed me for the better' and 'I feel so fulfilled at last' – the implication being that anything less than ultimate beatific fulfilment is for wimps. But at the same time, we will be able to slot it into our busy lives and march on regardless, Amazonians that we are. Succumbing to the confusion, emotional turmoil and life-change of motherhood is unacceptable. Nowadays, there's none of that wimpy lying around in bed whilst an ample-bosomed local hoovers the carpet and feeds you burnt stew, as would have happened in Nana's day — now it's a race to see which of us can sprint out the hospital doors the quickest. Accepting that motherhood might change you and change your priorities is simply not allowed.

Perhaps this might explain why, after so many years of hang-your-baby-around-your-neck-at-all-times advice, of encouraging parents to focus more on their babies' needs, old-fashioned guides to parenting babies are coming back into fashion, with their crisp advice on placing 'baby' in his/her cot at scheduled times, and only allowing him/her to sleep for twenty minutes at precisely 16.23. And then there are magazines with their advice on how to look 'fabulous' after you've had a baby, with their blithe suggestions as to how to squeeze feet into high heels to look your best for your husband in case he might think that you've let standards slip since you've had a baby. These echo our desire to package motherhood into a nice, clean, safe box with a shiny designer bow on it, and get on with the rest of our lives.

In Ireland, breastfeeding is considered to be the preserve of hairy-armpitted, basket-on-the-front-of-bicycle vegan earth-mother types, and I have got the distinct impression from some that it is just too much trouble. I met a friend recently who had just had a baby and who had switched to a bottle for the night-time feeds. And what's wrong with that? It was her 'A good night's sleep is very important,' that got me, as if I didn't know.

Fortunately, she was oblivious to my gnashed teeth as I tried to remain civil. Surely, if you'd had a baby, you weren't supposed to get 'a good night's sleep'. I felt like a mug. For some, I know sleep is something they are not prepared to give up to a baby and that's fair enough, even though I want to kill them.

And yet, on the other hand, many of the baby-centred edicts of the likes of *Breast or Death* imply that no sacrifice is too much for our beloved children and that we must lay ourselves out on the altar of their needs, resulting in impossibly high expectations of ourselves. I have made many of the classic mistakes of the liberal, wishy-washy mum – carrying 'Baby' – they are always called 'Baby' – around all the time, feeding him plentifully whilst eating lots of chocolate, and not letting him/her out of my sight for any length of time. But there we go: I adopted my own strategies for coping with the early days, such as copious amounts of walking; attempting to eat standing up so as not to wake baby, often finding a little head showered in cake crumbs when I got home; placing them in front of *Neighbours*, the theme tune to which seemed to invite a pleasant little slumber; bathing them regularly simply to wear them out; and popping them in between my husband and myself, to ensure a half-decent night's sleep. This was particularly helpful with my daughter, who wouldn't go to sleep before 3 a.m., but who would cheerfully lie in the dark in between us, gurgling away until eventually she succumbed to sleep. (A friend used to be able to get two hours' peace from her daughter by putting her cot mobile on repeat, even if she was demented by the tinny sound of *My Favourite Things* coming from the bedroom.) The interesting thing is that many of the books I slavishly consulted didn't actually help, except to remind me of all the things I was doing wrong, with notable exceptions, such as Sheila Kitzinger's warm *First Year of Motherhood*, which was like a hug from a big-bosomed granny, all powdery and reassuring and Penelope Leach, a woman of brisk good sense and a firm directness.

It was from my mother and mother-in-law that I learned about mothering of a more instinctive kind. Both of them came to stay for a week or so to help out, both in practical ways – 'I've emptied the laundry basket!' my mother would shout triumphantly every couple of days, and there was much washing, making dinner, giving out about how terrifying London was – but they also prodded me gently towards more confident caring for my baby. Whilst some of their advice was a bit toe-curling – leaving him to 'cry it out', winding him in a way that would make him vibrate, suggesting spoonfuls of Guinness for consti- pation – they handled the baby with the kind of firm and gentle confidence that I admired and tried to emulate. My mother-in-law was a great woman for swaddling babies and, in spite of my protests, wrapped my son up tight in his blanket, like a Russian babushka – I'm surprised she didn't find a coat-hook to hang him on while she was at it – and off he went to the land of Nod, without even a murmur. My mother was an expert at rocking a baby to sleep and after a bit of her gentle shushing and patting, off he'd go again. It turned out that the previous generation had something to teach me after all.

But sometimes I had to fight with them to assert myself and my own instincts about what I felt was right for my baby: both found the idea of breastfeeding exclusively a bit mystifying: would I not make life a bit simpler for myself if I gave him the odd bottle? To me, rabid breastfeeder that I was, this was heresy. And whilst I insisted on carrying him around, they would both mutter darkly about how I was making a rod for my own back; that he'd never want to settle down by himself and in their day babies were left in their prams for hours. In this, they had a point – up until the age of two my son was still raising his arms and demanding to be carried – but I bit back the urge to blame the woes of my generation on the fact that babies were to be kept at a safe distance, sleeping nicely in their cots, 'airing' their lungs for long periods and not receiving vast amounts of attention.

What I learned from my mother was that both of us were 'natural' in our own ways, my mother in her gentle confidence and calm reassurance and me in my overdone but sincere efforts to provide all that I could for my baby, and to follow my own instincts.

I had to learn for myself how to be a mother, but I needed help and support from others, from my bemused husband, who would walk the streets of Islington, baby in a sling, to allow me to catch up on some sleep, to my lovely health visitor and the midwives who 'popped in' for a month after the birth – the kind of support that my mother would not have had. I spent the next four months of my son's life sitting around under the dripping trees in Highbury or Victoria Park or around a kitchen table in Stoke Newington, or in the very spacious mother-and-baby rooms in John Lewis department store, talking utter nonsense with my fellow mothers. I discovered that one put her baby to sleep on her tummy, because the baby liked that best; another insisted on a cot in a different room because she simply couldn't sleep with the shuffling and the rustling and the general Darth Vader-like sounds her baby made; another didn't bathe the baby because as she rightly – pointed out, babies don't get dirty, only their tiny bottoms, and so the nightly bath was not necessary, and in fact dried their skin out. Through my friends I learned of the usefulness of aqueous cream, cot mobiles, driving around the block to soothe a screaming baby, drinking wine to promote better breastfeeding – it works, really, as long as you are not completely sloshed. I also learned that others didn't find motherhood a breeze and were fumbling their way through it, just like me.

Eventually, my life began to take on a new shape. So none of my clothes were left unmarked by baby sick, and I hadn't read anything more challenging than *Hello!*, but I had managed to find some kind of equilibrium and acceptance of my new life. Sure, I wasn't going to be scaling Everest any time soon, with baby slung over my shoulder, but I could at least enjoy my life again, and my baby.

*

I suppose I should feel ashamed of the fact that I suffered from depression after the birth of my son. And, although it is a long time ago now, I still feel the urge to brush it away, to hide in the dusty cupboard of memory and not retrieve the feelings of mortification, embarrassment and sadness that went with my first attempts at motherhood. And yet, I suppose I learned something from my earlier experiences: that even in today's world, we can not defy nature by the force of sheer will and by the sophistication and wealth of our lives; and we can't defy motherhood – pretend that it won't change or shape us in any way, we can't conquer it in the way we do a difficult spreadsheet or a PowerPoint presentation: it is messy, not neat; instinctive, not learned; emotional, not rational. Perhaps we should listen to our mothers after all, to something earlier and primeval in our journey towards becoming mothers. And we should listen to ourselves.

Take It from Me

* If you find, as did I, that the weepiness and gloom of day three doesn't lift, tell someone. It's normal to feel harassed, weepy, in discomfort and bewildered by the whole post-birth process and the early days of your baby; but if you find that the cloud won't lift, that the effort of getting out of bed, or running a bath makes you weep, that your baby could smile for England/Ireland and you find it hard to smile back, that sometimes you feel anger that you literally can't control, seek help. Who knows why some of us become depressed and others don't – I suffered from depression, so the chances were high that I would suffer from some form of post-natal depression (PND), but thanks to the excellent supports available to me, I survived it. Second-guessing and blaming yourself will not get you better. Help will.

* Trust your instincts. This sounds like the kind of truism you'd encounter in one of those hand-woven guides to motherhood, but this is really the only advice you'll ever need. Dr Spock said it, and it remains true to this day. As mothers, our minds can get filled with all kinds of rubbish, a set of rules and regulations about sleeping, feeding, eating, wind,

walks, prams, cots, baby in/out of the bed, the right
time to wean, and so it goes on: you need to look at
your baby and listen to him/her and decide what's
right for you both. If he will only sleep in a
hammock, or with AC/DC on at full blast, so what?
You can fit him with earphones if the neighbours
complain. Similarly, if you think your baby is unwell,
listen to yourself and not to people telling you he/she
is perfectly fine, or if you think he needs more or less
than six feeds a day, go with what you feel is right,
not what such and such a book says. I learned this the
hard way, by trying everything that was 'wrong' for
my babies and being roundly rejected.

* My mother is a great believer in 'routine', in trying to
get babies and children into a regular pattern of eating
and sleeping, which makes them happier and more
relaxed, she feels. Her following of Dr Spock's advice
in this regard made the early days of her babies much
less traumatic and unpredictable. When she came to
stay with me, her placing of 'Baby' firmly in his cot
every so often worked a treat, although I was less
keen on her edict that he could happily 'air his lungs'
by roaring the house down. I felt that he was probably
trying to tell me something and would shoot her a
filthy look when she would urge me to leave him for
a bit to 'cry it out'. I do take her point, though,
about not needing to get hysterical every time they let

out a wail and that, sometimes, I might not be able to fix what ailed them.

* 'Sleep when your baby sleeps'. Ah, yes, the age-old mantra. I had stupidly thought I could get on with my life as before, doing my jobs, visiting friends, going to the bank, only this time with an adorable little baby in tow. I hadn't bargained for the fact that it would take me three hours to get out the door, what with feeding/changing/ feeding again because he's hungry again/changing the resulting poo/taking on or off the snowsuit, depending on the weather, wondering whether to bring the cot mobile with you to soothe him on the bus journey, taking some food in case you get stranded in some remote place unpopulated by another living soul, and hence shops. I eventually learned to ditch the preparations – in fact any sorties for at least three weeks – and fall asleep on the sofa at any opportunity.

* Breastfeeding is not easy – I have spent many a night in front of the telly, crying with discomfort, trying to encourage a restless, wriggling baby to take the breast – but it does get easier for both of you. You will get the hang of it as long as you get them to open their mouths like the jaws of death, and press them to your bosom as if you intend to smother them. Don't worry about people telling you to take them off after ten

minutes because they don't 'need' any more milk.
If you want to stick them on all day while you watch
reruns of *Bonanza*, so what?

* For milk production and all-round relaxation for those
difficult night-time feeding sessions, you can't beat a
glass of wine and a little snooze just before teatime.
Easier said than done, I know, but snooze and booze
is a sure-fire winner. I wish I had drunk more, instead
of virtuous bloody water – although, to be fair, you
do need plenty of that, too.

* Ignore the baby schedulers, who don't believe that
motherhood will change them one iota. They won't
succumb to the biscuit tin, the toddler group or
This Morning. How utterly pathetic. As educated
professional women, they will simply sail through
feeding, changing and sleepless nights, getting baby
into a routine at four days and marching off to rule a
small country, book theatre tickets and host a dinner
party for forty. Motherhood is not a competitive
sport, so ignore this kind of nonsense, and trust what
you want to do, when you want to do it.

* Freeze vast amounts of food and buy lots of instant
meals as, if you are breastfeeding, you will be
ravenous, but will not be able to 'create' anything
more nourishing than toasted cheese sandwiches.

Chapter Four

A Hand Grenade into a
Marriage: Motherhood and
My Relationship

'As most members will know, our organiser Ena O'Reilly was married in August and is now Mrs Fox.'

Irish Countrywomens Association,
Minutes of Regional Meeting, Ennis, 1958

'Another man told me that he was sitting watching television late one night after his wife had gone upstairs for bed. "After a while," he said, "she came down again and threw the door open and announced, 'I'm fed up with you being unromantic, always watching television. Don't you ever feel like courting me any more?' She was dressed," he continued drily, "in a nightie which she had on our honeymoon five years ago. It had scorch marks and holes in it. She had a cardigan with only one button left on it over that and her hair in rollers. Her face was covered in some cream or other. It was all a perfect picture of romance!"'

Dorine Rohan, *Marriage, Irish-Style*, Mercier, 1969

When Nana died nine years ago, my mother gave me quite a few of her things, many of which had been wedding presents. A magpie like myself, Nana hadn't been wealthy enough to collect art or anything posh, but I loved her set of hand-painted placemats, her Limoges cake stand and her rather vulgar gold-painted tea set. I saw the knick-knacks as a good omen, souvenirs of a happy marriage which had given me the blueprint for my own.

This eulogy is not to imply for a moment that I have a perfect marriage. Like many couples, we can't stand each other in a million small ways – my husband wonders why I have to break anything that I come into contact with, racing through life at breakneck speed, a whirlwind of impatience and angst whilst his methodical way of doing things makes me want to scream loudly, rip whatever it is out of his hand and do it, *quickly*. He, on the other hand, must spend his life trying to stay ahead of whatever daft idea I'm going to come up with now, nodding his head as I rant on about how perfect it would be to live in

Portugal – imagine, the kids would be fluent in Portuguese! – and trying to keep a suitably neutral tone in his voice, just enough to let me run out of steam without encouraging me in any way. I must endure his sometimes maddening caution – whilst accepting that without it we would probably be penniless and living under a flyover with our three lovely children – as well as the constant succession of damp towels on the bed and DIY tools lying around, from a man who is remarkably fastidious in every other way. He has accepted that, unlike him, I am dizzily inefficient when it comes to matters domestic, eschewing the hoovering for another lovely novel, my children having been trained into wearing odd socks, and the house being covered in what I consider a perfectly acceptable layer of dust.

As we settle into the middle period of our relationship, we trundle along, unable to agree on the correct way to handle the credit crisis, or which series of *The Wire* is the best, but still more-or-less intact. After the upheavals of our children's early lives we have settled into a comfortable pattern, but the smug plateau of middle-aged marriage has been hard won. We have had to face some harsh truths about our relationship, about how well we have adapted to having children, how we have negotiated the new roles this has thrust upon us and the new realities we face. And, unlike my parents and grandparents, who clung to the certainties of their well-defined roles, we have had to make our parenting roles up as we go along, constantly shifting and changing as the children grow and as our own needs change. We have had to face the fact that with increasing equality comes increasing complexity, and have questioned whether equality is attainable at all. When Nora Ephron referred to having a baby being like tossing a hand grenade into a marriage, she was right.

*

All marriages begin with the expectation of a long and happy life together, and our expectations are largely romantic ones – of a life-long passion, a unique bond, a happy-ever-after fairytale straight out of *Barbie Princess*. One of my favourite things to do as a child was to look at my mother's wedding photos, or to ask her to tell me the story – for the hundredth time – of how she met Dad; I would examine the black-and-white photos of her 'looking triumphant' as our daft Uncle Neil used to say, in her broderie anglaise wedding gown and neat pillbox head-dress, and at the fuzzy brown-tinted ones of my Nana, in her plain brown suit, unable to afford a wedding dress, and see the many happy years that followed for both of them. Nana would get misty-eyed as she recalled her courtship with Granddad, as he escorted her home from her job in Cassidy's clothes shop on Georges Street to her home in Harold's Cross, before cycling the quarter mile or so on to his lodgings in the Georgian splendour of Kenilworth Square. This would have to be done before the nightly curfew, a legacy of the Civil War which still clung on in newly independent Ireland. I remember thinking this was terribly romantic when Nana had told me as an impressionable teenager, the two of them cycling home along the canal with the odd crack of gunfire in the background . . .

To secure Nana's hand, Granddad would have to use every ounce of fortitude at his disposal, to extract her from her large dependent family and clingy mother who would create a pressing family drama generally involving one of Nana's wayward younger brothers every time it looked like Nana might leave to get married. Widowed from an early age, Nana's mother had found herself destitute with eight children to clothe and feed. Unable to cope, she came to rely on Nana as both wage earner and substitute head of the family – the idea that this might be taken away was simply too much for her. As a result, Nana married at the comparatively ancient age of twenty-seven, in 1936. And this only after Granddad Jack had finally snapped and issued an ultimatum: him or her mother. Either Nana married him right away, or he was off to Arklow to his first posting as a social welfare officer – alone. With the mother of the bride not speaking to anyone, Nana and Granddad were married at the Temperance Hotel off Harcourt Street, an alcohol-free venue selected to please the groom's teetotal father, and honeymooned in Connemara.

My mother met my father at a 'hop' at a local rugby club, to which she'd gone with a friend. It was Ladies'

Choice and my mother strode out on the dance floor to claim her partner, only to be beaten to the punch by another girl. 'And your father was standing just behind him,' she told me, rolling her eyes to heaven, as if to imply that he wasn't her first choice, which, although strictly true, we both know to be a happy lie. And that was that, too. There were no nightmare mothers-in-law in this scenario, unless you count Nana, whom my father tolerated extremely well, even though she had tried to poison him with dodgy trifle on his first Christmas with the in-laws. There was a lovely wedding in January 1963, in the snow, and a cheerful reception at a Dublin hotel, and a wedding photo in the *Irish Times*. They were a nice middle-class couple embarking on their lives together and they looked entirely happy about it. Now, I look at my own wedding photos, my rosy twenty-five-year-old features in my rather-late-eighties choice of shiny purple dress with prominent shoulder pads and chunky jewellery and even shinier tights – tan with a dusting of gold, as I remember, complete with sock marks around my ankles, as I'd been wearing a tracksuit until an hour beforehand. My husband's thick black curls fall over his forehead and his navy blue suit is almost too big for his narrow frame. We both look like the college students we were until a couple of years beforehand; children in our Sunday best, cutting our wedding cake.

*

In order to marry in the Catholic church, which we did in order not to upset our parents – we weren't quite old enough or confident enough to want to annoy them by tying the knot in the Little White Chapel of Elvis or at a limbo-dancing ceremony in the Caribbean – we had had to undertake a 'pre-marriage course'. These are mandatory, and although every couple scoffs at them, they still shuffle off to the priest's house for a couple of Saturdays to prepare for marriage by reflecting on some of the issues and challenges that lie ahead.

As my husband and I were getting married in Dublin but living in London, we had to repair to the parish house in Archway, just after Sunday Mass. The priest barrelled in from the church, brown anorak over his vestments, a vigorous, cheerful man with a brisk manner. Cigarette in hand, he enquired as to whether he'd seen us at Sunday Mass at all? We gazed at him blankly, having been in the local café eating a fry-up until moments before. Shrugging his shoulders, he proceeded to inform us that as all the pre-marriage courses were full, we'd have to make do with a blessing. Puffing away on his cigarette, he muttered something about 'going together towards God', and with a brisk smile, signed us off. That was it. We were 'ready' to be married.

At the time, we laughed at having got away without the tedium of the preparations, but now I wonder. When I got married – after all the fuss and the preparations, the bridezilla carry-on about the hideous Bay City Rollers carpet that adorned the function room and a day-long fit of hysterics about finding exactly the right kind of shoe to match the purple dress — I thought that marriage was a love story, a perfect moment which would last until we were eighty-five, when we should shuffle off into the sunset together, as much in love as we had been on the day we married. Now, of course, I realize just how utterly daft that idea is; that the wedding is only the tip of the iceberg, and what may begin as a love story becomes something else entirely; that life together is a constant battle in some ways, a negotiation of needs and roles and desires, a constant compromise and accommodation of someone else, which goes on every single day long after you have stopped gazing moonily into each other's eyes and shagging at every opportunity.

And, most importantly, that children will generally come along and make you focus on every difference you ever had. The needs of your adorable baby will turn you either permanently or temporarily into your mother and him into a newspaper-wielding throwback to the 1940s, will leave you both struggling to work out what roles you must both play, now that lover and best friend must take a back seat to those of Mum and Dad, will make you wonder if, having spent every waking moment together in blissful harmony, you will ever do anything together ever again, apart from bark commands about putting the bins out and changing nappies; whether the person who once meant 'everything' to you will ever do so again. Perhaps

a week or two reflecting on this might not have done us
any harm.

*

But at the time, everything was so *perfect*. I had sneaked
into my husband's lodgings in Islington, into the two huge
and faintly gloomy adjoining rooms he rented from the
fearsome Mrs George, who laundered his sheets every
week and kept a very close eye on goings-on; with its
single gas ring per room, communal showers and luridly
patterned wallpaper, it housed a number of single men in
vests and Y-fronts, some more peculiar than others. We
couldn't have been happier, sitting on his plastic-covered
black armchair, plates of rice and pork chop on our knees,
watching the *Brookside* omnibus on his tiny black-and-
white TV. Alone in London without family, we relied on
each other and lived our lives together in every way. Life
was simple then: my husband wrote every evening after
work whilst I watched TV in the room next door and
listened to the man upstairs playing the drums and the
couple across the road fighting, and tried to get our lovely
downstairs neighbour to turn down Rick Astley. I even
tolerated my husband's fortnightly fishing trips with his
mates – probably because they really *were* fishing trips,
i.e. they put bait at the end of a fishing line and sat for an
entire day waiting to catch something; they weren't
euphemisms for drinking lots of pints and watching football. Sometimes, if the weather was good, I even went

with him, stockpiling Sunday supplements to while away the hours on the riverbank whilst he watched a float bobbing up and down in the water. My husband and I congratulated ourselves that our marriage was truly modern: we both worked and shared everything equally, our crappy media salaries, the household chores and shopping and all of the stuff of our lives. I looked up to my husband as a potential literary giant and admired the sacrifices he made for his work – he was my hero and I offered him my unwavering support. There was an equilibrium which, we happily told ourselves, could withstand anything, a balance which, until now, hadn't been challenged in any real way.

*

And then my son came along and turned all of those smug assumptions on their heads.

*

When Ian was born, unlike many macho Irish dads, my father was happy to push him in his pram up and down the local seafront: 'It was quite unusual at the time,' Mum told me, 'because only English people did that.' To the unreconstructed Irish, the English were considered to be terribly advanced, and my father had learned from the example of his English family, but this emphatically did not make him a New Man: although he was a 'great man for helping out', fundamentally his role as breadwinner, as head of the family, did not change, and nor did my mother's as stay-at-home mother, carer and housewife. When my son was born, within the space of a year we went from husband and wife to mother and father, in my case from working woman to unemployed new mum, in my husband's from part-time to full-time writer and from swinging Islington to a deserted, out-of-season seaside town near Dublin. It was quite a 'land', as we say here. And unlike my parents, neither of us was entirely sure what was expected of us in this brave new world.

In London it appeared that we had somehow managed to accommodate the necessary changes in our relationship in familiar surroundings, or maybe it was just that we could ignore the fact that things had changed. We were still able to book a table in Pizza Express at the Angel, this time taking our baby with us, although as he would only sleep in a sling, eating a pizza involved having to balance him carefully on our knees and snarf it, trying not to drop hot tomato sauce on his little head; we could still have friends around for a drink or a bowl of pasta, but would have to raise our voices to drown out the pro-longed screaming fit between seven and eight every evening as my son's colic reached its zenith and he would have to be held and soothed to distract him from the pain. We were harassed and sleep-deprived and, with our 'me-time' taking a severe bashing, constantly watching each other to make sure neither of us got more than our fair share – did my husband have 3.5 seconds more than his allotted half an hour in front of *Match of the Day*? Had I been in the bath for a few minutes too long? Who changed his nappy the last time, or got up to soothe him back to sleep, or to bathe him? Trips out of the house would be planned and executed with the furtive cunning of the CIA operative, in case the other person would get wind of the planned trip to Sainsbury's for a giant pack of nappies and succumb to a fit of jealous rage. 'Going *out*? That's nice,' one of us would mutter through clenched teeth, silently fuming.

And of course, being an over-anxious mother eager to prove herself, I often ignored my husband in favour of my son. Whereas before I had been only too eager to hear how my husband's day had gone, now I often bustled past him, martyred expression on my face, to make dinner, but not before thrusting the baby into his arms like an unexploded scud missile. I would spend entire evenings cooing and fussing over the baby – was he too hot or too cold, was he dry enough, should I change his nappy before or after his feed, and what about a bath, had he eaten enough, farted enough, burped enough? On one occasion I ordered my husband to turn off *The Godfather: Part II*, which he'd happily been watching, as the scene where the helicopter gunfire rains down on the mafiosi through the Las Vegas hotel ceiling would traumatize the baby, aged five weeks. I would often change the baby's nappy, not forgetting to throw my husband a filthy look whilst I did so, as by doing so I would score martyr points, instead of simply asking him to do it. He later revealed that he had simply given up trying to offer help, as when he did, he would be fixed with a glare: only I, my look seemed to say to him, was properly able to care for our son. My husband, once the light of my life, had been replaced by a new and beguiling focus, whose need of me was total. My husband could look after himself. Nature can be cruel to a marriage.

However, neither of us realized that the real adjustments to being parents had yet to be made. We were too busy organizing our move back to Dublin after ten years, booking movers and urging them not to spill a full drawer of my knickers onto the street whilst loading the chest of drawers into the van, finishing off work commitments as my husband bade a cheery farewell to the firm of chartered surveyors who had employed him for the previous ten years, and a slightly less cheery farewell to his fishing mates, who had so entertained us. And suddenly, there we were, in a rented mews in a seaside town outside Dublin. We felt we had landed on Mars. This place was completely uninhabited during the winter months by anyone other than heroin addicts – it seemed a long way from our days in Swinging Islington, hanging out in trendy cafés, *Guardian* clasped to our bosoms. The Little Gem newsagents on the windblown seafront had to order the *Guardian* in for us, and I had to queue for my coffee – 'White or black, love?' – behind a line of Latvian builders rebuilding the seafront, the sound of 'Hit Me

Baby One More Time' continually ringing in my ears from the tinny radio. From hanging out in wine bars in Soho, to Mr Chippy on Patrick Street, surrounded by people with sucked-in cheeks clad in the junkie's ensemble of choice, a white tracksuit.

My husband found himself pushing a buggy along the Dublin coast for miles, which many would think was a wonderful change of pace, but was disorienting in the extreme if you've been used to a rigid structure every day – the holiday can only last for so long. In the meantime, I had my sights set on a new working life, but I found that Irish publishers were less than receptive to my blandishments and my CV – did they know me? No. Had I come recommended by Jim O'Brien down the road? No. My plans for a new and exciting career as a portfolio worker were scuppered, due to the distinct lack of a portfolio. All of our ambitious plans for our return to Dublin in triumph, to the bosom of our families, seemed to fall flat. Of course, now I realize that building an entirely new life takes time and patience, of which I do not possess much, but then it simply looked as if our dreams were just that: dreams.

*

On the face of it, our problems were minor; our little challenges seem so mundane compared to those my parents and grandparents faced, when I compare them to the nine years of grief, anxiety and disappointment that

Nana must have endured and the end of her dream of having a proper 'family'. In the same way, it took Mum and Dad some time to realize that all was not well with my older brother. He was such a happy baby, smiling and content, sitting out in the garden in his floppy sun bonnet, a puppy or two popped in the pram with him for company, from the family dog Fancy's new litter. It was when he was two that the problems seemed to emerge. My mother had gone into hospital to have me and Ian went to Nana and Granddad's for two weeks' holiday. When my mother came home, Nana and Granddad drove up from Waterford with my brother in the back of the car. At the sight of his mother, he didn't bounce out of the car and run up for a hug, but wandered cautiously into the house and took in his surroundings before pointing to his mother and saying, 'Am I going to stay with this lady now?' Bewildered and hurt, Mum had no idea that this would be the beginning of a lifetime's work as his autism became more apparent and the smiling easy baby became an obsessive, uncommunicative little boy. She would spend her every waking moment trying to keep him safe from the scrapes and escapades that were part of his early years, and which have become favourite stories with my children – the Time Uncle Ian Hijacked a Pedal Car and Pushed it Four Miles, The Time Uncle Ian Dived into the Neighbours' Pond – but which must have been a nightmare for them. Then there was the physical aggression towards other children, which would leave her both isolated and with the label of 'bad mother' attached firmly to her, compounded by the constant fight to get him the kind of education he needed when no one saw any compelling reason why he should get one at all. And yet, my parents' marriage was, or always appeared to be, rock solid, separate from and impermeable to Ian's antics. If anything, the challenges seemed to make their marriage stronger.

Having a baby, moving back home and doing essentially new jobs doesn't seem that big a deal, and yet it was enough to shift the basis on which we had built our marriage, tilting it on its axis, leaving us temporarily unanchored, with nothing more than the length of our relationship to keep us afloat. Our oldest child seemed to blast a hole in our close compatibility, leaving us both reeling and unsure what, if our relationship was changing, it might now be. In addition, we had gone from being two people who had forged our own life in London to our parents' son and daughter, our siblings' brother and sister. In London we could be whomever we liked – if I wanted to pierce my nose and wear a mohican, no one would have cared. At home, my husband and I quickly assumed our old roles. For our families we would forever be the reliable pair, him with his pliers and spanner ready to help with lawnmower repair and computer problems, me relaying information to my younger sister that my mother regarded as sensitive and dropping in to see Nana to try to persuade her to get a hearing aid or to stop driving.

Returning home to Dublin seemed to throw our differences into relief and we felt that our problems had their root cause in our return home. Things would have been just fine if we had stayed in London, we moaned. But of course, they wouldn't – the move really drove underground the massive changes that becoming a parent had wrought and the renegotiation of roles that now needed to take place.

*

Marriage, during my parents' and grandparents' time, was not a partnership of equals. Both Nana and Mum married men who were described as being 'very good to them'. 'I know men who beat their wives and ran off to the pub every night,' my mother told me. 'And I was so glad that I'd found a man who wasn't like that.' My father was reliable, kind and happy to hand over his wages to my mother every week and to have his spending money doled out to him by a woman whom he knew to be more sensible with money than he was. Out of his spending money he would pay for his pints in the pub or sailing club, or the rugby club on match day. He would dig troughs for potatoes in the vegetable garden, take rubbish to the dump, prune the apple trees and other masculine activities; and he would also cook: elaborate steak dinners and Chinese stir-fry beef at the weekends, but that was the extent of his encroachment into my mother's territory. All other things to do with us were my mother's preserve: the house was her office and, crucially, they had agreed early on in their marriage that my mother would actively manage Ian's needs, with Dad's support. 'Ian put a lot of strain on us,' my mother agreed, 'but we never disagreed or rowed – we'd discuss it. Dad let me get on and look after Ian, but he supported and encouraged me. He does feel guilty sometimes that I took on too much, but I had the time to do it, and it was my job.' The boundaries were clear: theirs was a real partnership, but each knew what the other's job was.

In Nana's marriage, however, Jack was clearly in control. 'Your grandfather put women on a pedestal,' Mum told me. 'He liked them to have long hair and wear nice clothes.' And there was also something of a Pygmalion vibe as Granddad tried to get Nana to share in his autodidactic pleasures: he'd get very excited if he got her to read anything, exclaiming to my mother, 'She finished a book, isn't that great?' even if it was nothing more than the latest Vicki Baum, the Barbara Taylor Bradford of her day. He decided that Nana didn't need to drive – why would she, when he could take her everywhere? – or work, or adopt children to replace the family she had lost, and Nana – despite having a very strong personality – acquiesced in all of this without a murmur. Having been responsible for her own family her entire life she was quite happy to be looked after for a bit, but whatever the reasons, this hair-raising inequality worked for them.

In Nana and Granddad's marriage, the division of labour was clear, to the extent that Jack couldn't cook anything other than the most basic meals for himself and had to rely on his landlady to come in and make his dinner when Nana was visiting her mother in Dublin. On one occasion, when the landlady didn't appear, he was reduced to serenading the hens in the hen-house at the bottom of the garden in the hope that an egg might be forthcoming. In my marriage, although the roles are fairly traditional, it is understood that all activities, with the exception of putting the bins out, for which I am happy to surrender my feminist principles, are up for grabs. My husband drops the kids to school on his way to work and is happy to wield a Hoover. We have a joint account which we are happy to share as there isn't much in it in any case. I cook during the week simply because I am there, and I sometimes snort with laughter at his weekend 'event' cooking, whilst eating his porcini risotto with relish. He cleans the kitchen to a clinical degree: if he had committed murder, CSI would not glean a trace of forensic evidence in our kitchen after he's been over it with the Mr Muscle. We make all decisions to do with the children as a couple, and my husband wouldn't dream of suggesting that I not work or drive a car. But we have also done things the other way around: for the first six years of our children's lives it was he who stayed at home with the children and I who got up on my bicycle every morning to go off to work in the office: the effects on our marriage were interesting.

After a couple of years freelancing, I was offered a job at a local publishing firm. To say I grabbed it with both hands was an understatement. Our financial needs in Shiny New Ireland had become too great. We'd bought a house much closer to town, and practically ran out of the seaside town, barely waving goodbye, but the mortgage still needed to be paid, and so our ideal of sharing our time and providing the perfect environment for our son ended. It was decided that my husband would stay at home and I would take advantage of meeting the first publisher who'd displayed any enthusiasm about my arrival from the UK, like Jesus come back from the dead. By this stage, my son was a toddler and my daughter had come along, a dainty, tiny girl who was so quiet I hadn't even realized that I was pregnant with her for the first three months. A surprise baby, she is the light of my life.

Looking back, this was the most difficult period of our marriage. On paper, it all seemed to make sense. I was earning a regular income and my husband continued to get lump sums for his writing, and he was able to be at home with our small children: he always loved the baby and toddler years while I found them disorienting. He was happy to push the buggy for miles and to make sandcastles with them or to bring them out to B&Q and push them around on the huge flatpack trolley, in search of tile grouting and garden gravel, or if he wasn't, I didn't ask him. After three or four years at home, I was dying to get out back into the world and, although I missed storytime and Play-Doh, I embraced the new job with relish.

But, even with us both working at full tilt, there never seemed to be enough money. Everyone else was driving around in new-reg cars, shiny new Volkswagen Beetles and Minis, not the old ones we would have been happy to chug around in ten years previously. Everyone except us. And even if we weren't terribly bothered about our eight-year-old white Fiat Punto, we might as well have been wearing a sign around our necks: 'Celtic Tiger Failures', not cut-and-thrusty enough to make it as property developers and therefore consigned to ride bicycles around the city like throwbacks to the peasant era. And even though I had a new job, with all the responsibilities and expectations that went with it, the feeling of being the Great Hope of the firm, I was only being paid a part-time salary until my stable of authors built up enough for me to merit full-time hours, and my husband was free-lancing around the children, which meant that we were more broke than ever. Our daily and weekly lives became a ritual of penny-counting and hidden frustration, the constant, gnawing anxiety of wondering where the next penny would come from, to get us past the next electricity bill or grocery shop.

And so, as the months wore on and the strain began

to show, quite naturally we began to take it out on each other. Could my husband not get a job? I nagged . . . and nagged . . . and nagged. Well, no, in spite of everything, he couldn't. There wasn't much demand for writers in Bank of Ireland and we were both committed to raising our children as best we could, i.e. with one of us staying at home. Perhaps this was ridiculously naive, but it was such a priority that we were prepared to make the necessary sacrifices. So what if we lived in a fever of marital tension half the time? The kids were happy, weren't they? Well, yes, but I was still determined to beat him over the head about it.

In our marriage, the more-or-less equal partnership had been replaced by something different. It was a battle to see who had the greater 'responsibility'. I had the regular salary, but always struggled with the fear and anxiety of being responsible for the family financially: my job was experimental, a new initiative for a conservative firm, and I would torture myself with 'what-if' scenarios. What if I lost my job and the family was destitute? By the same token, my husband seemed to lose himself for a while, his self-confidence battered by the realities of writing full-time and discovering that it wasn't all it was cracked up to be. Was the person with the money the important one? I am ashamed to say it, but I didn't value my husband's work at home: where was the man whom I had always looked up to as being somehow bigger and stronger than I? I felt like a martyr, the grumpy dad in the suit with my husband cast as the depressed housewife. Our uncomplicated time together in London now seemed like another lifetime, along with the people we once were to each other. We were now ships passing in the kitchen or bedroom, the once-eager conversation about writing, books, films and music now muttered banalities about the 'to-do' list for the day.

On the face of it, things slowly improved financially as my job grew and his freelance career as a copywriter took off, but there was still something that wasn't right. We had tried sharing parenting equally, reversing the roles, but it didn't quite fit. I knew that I had been handed an opportunity in my job, but also that I hadn't come back to Dublin to return to my old life, with its lengthy commute and the boredom of office life, and yet I couldn't put my finger on what possible alternatives there might be. And my husband found that being at home with small children was, well, boring, all the more so, because, as a man, he found himself excluded from the cosy playground chats, from the sense of community and support extended to mothers in the same situation, and which is often the only thing that keeps them going. When the other mothers would see him coming, they wouldn't exactly scatter, but nor would they invite him to discuss their book group's choice of reading material, or to share the swimming class rota. And mothers were reluctant to arrange playdates with Dad in charge, prefer-ring to text me, or not to arrange playdates at all. My husband used to spend an awful lot of time in B&Q, or putting up shelving. Ireland, unlike trendy metropolitan London, wasn't ready for the stay-at-home dad.

It was when my youngest son was born, a pugnacious little man who entertained and terrified us in equal measure, that the penny dropped. My mother-in-law asked me one day if I was looking forward to returning to work and I answered truthfully: 'No, and it wouldn't bother me if I never did.' I ignored her look of astonishment. I used to be a sucker for the cut-and-thrust of office life, the little rituals of chat and bicker, the water-cooler conversations, the jousting in the editorial meeting, but now that old restless spirit seemed to have gone; I wanted to try something new, and, whisper it, to spend more time at home with the children. Here I was, like many women before me, realizing that I couldn't, didn't want to, have it all, at least not for a little while.

And so, with infinite patience and kindness, my husband agreed to support me whilst I found what I was looking for. He smiled politely as I waved brochures for charity treks through Namibia and various entrepreneurial ideas at him and complained about how boring life was at home with the kids. And eventually, when I returned to writing after a number of years, he encouraged and prompted and gave me the time to work, happy for me to closet myself in the bedroom and work away, snatching brief moments when the kids weren't awake/ill/fighting/ needing food to piece together something that wasn't a thriller set in a swimming pool. 'Why?' I asked him one day, when I'd had enough of redrafting chapter two forty-nine times and threw down my pen in frustration. 'Well, it's clearly important to you,' he replied mildly, adjusting his fantasy football team on the laptop and muttering under his breath that Lampard was off again. He was right, it was important, but without his encouragement, I would never have done anything about it except day-dream. Clearly, he is a better person than I.

And, to my slight shame, the traditional roles seem to suit our household at this juncture in our lives. I feel almost guilty saying it, as if it is a betrayal of every *Guardian*-reading instinct, but it's true in my case. I like this time of my children's lives and the fun and entertainment I get from hearing about their day and their theories on the world, whereas my husband loved the baby stage and misses their kisses and cuddles and sticky hands. I was and am happy to tolerate the requests for new cats, rabbits and budgies and to spend hours cleaning out hutches and buying bunny treats, because I like animals and my husband doesn't. And the balance in our relationship rather selfishly suits me – I like the new, dynamic him and he has been sweetly tolerant of my stay-at-home mothering experiment, although I know he would like to spend more time with the children.

Finally, after ten years of turbulence, we have reached the calmer waters of middle age and have accepted that we have priorities other than absolute equality. But we both know that all of this wonderful equilibrium comes at a cost: there is the tacit understanding that it's my turn to pursue my dreams whilst my husband slogs at the coalface. I have more time and space to enjoy life's quiet pleasures but he doesn't. And no, that's not fair, but that's the big secret about marriage: that the everlasting romance, hearts and flowers will be replaced by constant compromise and the idea that sometimes it isn't possible for both of you to get you want at the same time.

And there is always the subtext that the main wage earner somehow calls the shots: my husband would never dream of crashing in the door and demanding that I run the Hoover over the living room carpet, or iron the school polo shirts; he is happy to bring my son and a dozen friends to the cinema for a birthday outing without moaning that there's football on, but every time I buy a pair of shoes or a new T-shirt, I wave the receipt at my husband and provide him with a lengthy justification for the purchase, which he greets with a shrug of his shoulders. 'It's not *my* money, you know, it's ours.' But it's not, I want to howl, it's really *not*, just as I'm sure my mother said to my father, even as she was handing him over his weekly allowance. It's a symbol of how much more 'important' your life is than mine. The raised eyebrows about the electricity bill make me feel even more guilty because I am contributing less to paying them. There is a definite but subtle power imbalance, a sense that because my husband is out there in the world beating off the other savages that he is somehow 'in control' and we, circling around him in our domestic bubble, are not.

But that's the pay-off for the decisions we make: equality is shunned for domestic stability – in marriage, as in life, we can't have everything.

*

Of course, we know that the great ideal of romantic love just isn't enough to sustain a marriage, but the irony of it all is that at a time when marriage is under greater strain, our expectations of it are so high. Marriage to us now isn't simply a question of finding someone with their own teeth, a reasonable wage and a pleasant disposition, whom we have married in order to avoid the spectre of pregnancy outside marriage, but a soulmate, who will nourish us spiritually, and ideally fulfil our *Sex-and-the-City* fantasies of marrying a wealthy businessman. We expect that our partners will be everything to us, will give us the freedom to be ourselves and to explore our fundamental qualities as a human being whilst at the same time being a loyal source of support and encouragement. These are qualities that only superhumans could fulfil, and yet our Barbie Princess fantasies have led us to expect all of this, and an excellent sex life while we're about it. The effort of looking distinctly foxy, aged forty-six, when we'd much rather be sitting in our M&S tracksuits watching *Grand Designs*, and of keeping our sex lives fresh as a daisy – how about a little bondage, or a French maid's outfit –

is all a bit tiring when, after twenty years of marriage, we'd really rather tuck ourselves up in bed with a nice novel, but instead we have to squeeze our ageing, cellulited buttocks into Agent Provocateur and look interested.

My mother described getting married as the next step in her life after school, and then work: it was simply what she did next, along with most of her contemporaries, just as her mother had done before her. Marriage was a state of being, another stage in your life, which would bring great compatibility or great distress, depending on your luck, a state in which children were expected automatically, not chosen carefully, where romantic love was not an expectation but a hope. Marriages like mine, so much freer and more open, more equal, are also more complicated and carefully balanced, with our children's needs equal to ours. To offer love and support takes a greater effort and an acknowledgement of the fact that marriage, rather than eternal love, is really a deep-seated psychological tussle for fulfilment, the ultimate test of our abilities to live with each other totally – not just for the nice bits.

*

This idea of true compromise is all the more necessary nowadays, when family life has changed so much. I decided to read John Updike's *Couples* recently, in a fit of guilt that I hadn't read a single Updike during his lifetime, and whilst enjoying the gin-slinging, capri-pants-wearing, arch-comment-making locals, I was amused and slightly shocked by the picture of middle-class parenthood that emerged in 1968 Connecticut: on returning home from a dinner party, the woman in a married couple remarks to her husband that their children are suffering because of their social lives, that perhaps they might be fed up getting dragged along in their parents' social wake, that in this small new England town, their fear that their friends might do something without them led to them neglecting their own children and their needs. This idea seems vaguely hilarious to us now, devoting as we do our entire beings to our children's fulfilment and happiness.

Nana and Granddad used to spend much of their spare time — and they had more-than-usual amounts of it, only having one child — hosting musical evenings, when friends would gather around the piano to sing cheerful Irish ballads, or less cheerful ones with forty-seven verses about sheep drowning when being rowed across the lake, which would bring a tear to every eye; and then there was the golf, which they discovered in Arklow and into which they threw themselves with gusto, loving every minute of the four-balls and cut crystal. My own parents spent a lot of time together, going to classical music concerts, literary evenings and even sailing, which my mother loathed, but tolerated in the name of togetherness, hiring a lovely local girl called Rosemary in her stripy tank top and flares to babysit us every Saturday afternoon. My parents wouldn't have dreamed of doing anything with us, apart from the

St Patrick's Day parade, when we would huddle in the sleet on O'Connell Street for a couple of hours, my mother muttering under her breath and trying to stop Ian from being crushed under the wheels of an agricultural float, or the day of our Holy Communion, when we would be taken out for chicken and chips followed by Neapolitan ice-cream. The rest of the time, we were on our own. Our parents took no huge interest in our hobbies: we made our way to and from piano lessons on our bikes and my mother is still complaining thirty-four years later about having had to drive me a mile to gym class every second Wednesday.

And then there were the drinks parties. Mum and Dad held one every St Stephen's Day, which the Irish refuse to call Boxing Day, when my father would do his annual hoover of the living room and my mother would instruct us to fill dishes with peanuts and crisps and order us not to eat a single thing. Dad would consult his long list of his guests' drinks requirements and mutter under his breath about getting extra tonic and murmur to Mum about how if Jim O'Daly from up the road was coming he'd better keep an eye on him and put the whiskey away after a bit, especially if he was driving. After lunch, couples just like those in *Couples* would gather in the hoovered and polished good room and drink large gin and tonics and we, dressed in our Sunday Mass outfits, would dutifully pass a dish of nuts around and be congratulated on what wonderful children we were and what class were we in now? Dad would allow us to help ourselves to unlimited fizzy drinks from the SodaStream, but it was clear that we were otherwise not to be seen. At an appointed time, my godfather, who was Dad's cousin and oldest friend, would appear in the kitchen, where we children were trying to keep out of our mother's way, clutching a blue Basildon Bond envelope in his hand with my name on it in neat blue ink, containing my Christmas present of a ten pound note. My memories of drinks-party purgatory are shared by most of my contemporaries, one of whom endured it on a weekly basis, every single Friday afternoon at her suburban home when the children would be herded together and practically thrown out into the back garden while their mothers drank very large cocktails, to be joined on their way home from work by their husbands. After many hours, the by-now consider-ably drunk parents would pile them all into a car and drive home.

How astonishing that seems nowadays, when we are all one big happy family in our open-plan kitchens, spending every weekend doing 'family stuff', boring ourselves rigid in the painting room at the art gallery with them, finding ourselves playing the bongos at the 'getting to know music' parent-and-toddler sessions at the parish hall when we'd really like to be tucking into a bucket of popcorn at the cinema with the kids firmly ensconced with the babysitter. Our social lives are devoted more or less entirely to our children, to cheering them on from the sidelines at football, to applauding their pirouettes at ballet and other achievements, and our lives as a couple are really squeezed into the margins. I can't think of a single thing that my husband and I do 'together', except put the kids to bed, as he wields the toothbrushes and I usher little bottoms into pyjamas. We occasionally manage a guerrilla, under-the-radar conversation about politics or the office when he gets in from work and the kids are absorbed in *The Simpsons*, but it is constantly interrupted by one child or another, alerted to the fact that their parents are – gasp – *together*. Of course we can get a babysitter, if we are prepared to spend a hundred euro on an outing to the pictures. Frankly, these days organizing an evening of togetherness requires the kind of effort that is all too easy to eschew. And Granny and Granddad, who would have been delighted to help out twenty years ago, now have to see if they can squeeze you in between bridge, the historical society, choir practice and scaling K2 single-handed with the Active Over-Seventies. It's easier just to let things slide and, unless you have a rock-solid foundation and an excellent memory for the romantic days of old to keep you warm, to fade away.

And so, we have to content ourselves with making time in small ways – having a chat when he comes in from work, insisting politely – or not so politely – that the children retire into the sitting room whilst we do so: 'Mummy and Daddy are *talking!*'; or we take the dreaded weekend break, arriving at our destination shadows of our former selves, having endured a 40-mile motorway tail-back or an airport delay, muttering to ourselves about it hardly being worth it, what with having had to organize single-handedly the Mongol Invasions, i.e. our children's schedules with Granny and Granddad, each of us eyeing the vast expanse of the white bed to see what's expected of us or if we can have a nice lie-down instead; or we go out for a meal or a drink and make vows not to talk about the children, which I find highly amusing: after eighteen years of marriage, and with our social lives not exactly energetic, there's not an awful lot else happening, is there? 'How's that tax return going?' 'Great!'

To be fair, my husband and I have a bond that has always sustained us and which we have rediscovered as the kids have grown older, and an interest in the world around us that provides us with grist to our conversational mill and staves off the awful spectre of cutlery scraping on china, although he does try to shoehorn in a comment or two about the Premiership which I studiously ignore, and he tries not to look terminally bored whilst I get excited about parents who overschedule their children and how many summer camps I should put them down for. I feel comfortable with the relative boredom of our couple-dom now, relieved that the fireworks are over, that equilibrium has been found: that we can both sit down together and chat idly about a subject without the background seethe, the well-worn mental laundry list running in our heads – why didn't he help with the baby when I did the washing up; why does he have all the fun when I'm stuck at home, etc. The smug assumptions of our early married life have been replaced by something more careful, less unequivocal and more grateful for each other and for the life we have.

Take It from Me

* If your relationship is basically sound, it will take a bashing when you have a baby and, for a while, you might 'forget' it. The needs of your partner won't seem half as important as those of your baby, and they're probably not; your partner is, after all, able to look after him/herself; but small kindnesses help to keep the doors open until such time as you can resurface. I wasn't very kind, to be honest, which is why I recommend it.

* Many people gush that 'our baby has brought us even closer together', which I find vaguely bewildering. I can't see how this could be, with one or both of you awake twenty-four hours a day, feeding, bathing, changing a baby. And the fact that you both revert to some post-war stereotypes can't help, as hubby rushes off to work whilst the Little Woman stays at home. Women can often be alarmed that their partner behaves just like his father, hiding behind the paper

and insisting on still playing five-a-side; men can often feel excluded from the golden circle of mother and baby and if she's breastfeeding, he can feel like a complete spare tool. Babies have a way of exposing every difference in your marriage, of upending, temporarily or sometimes permanently, long-cherished views of equality and sharing. A bonding experience it is not.

* Thankfully, this phase is mercifully not a permanent one, but the long-term renegotiations of roles and responsibilities are. Having a baby can make you – and your partner – rethink who you are in a profound way and can result in conflicts that you might not be able to resolve on your own. Getting help with this is not a sign of defeat.

* Often other upheavals go with having a baby, which can make a real dent in a relationship. For some reason, when we have a baby, we decide to make other stressful life changes like moving house or job, or country, as did we. With the benefit of hindsight, one upheaval would have done us nicely.

* When you are thinking about parenting responsibilities now that you have a baby, try to put 'traditional' ideas aside. For men, putting out a wash, making

dinner or taking your baby to the park won't diminish your manhood; if anything, women like a man who is in touch with his feminine side: it can introduce a welcome bit of danger to the mother-and-toddler coffee morning. For women, being desperate to escape the confines of home and buggy doesn't make you unfeminine, just someone who needs something else besides your gorgeous baby. Hanging on to elderly ideas about roles can keep you stuck and unhappy in roles that, these days, you need no longer adhere to.

* Many of the advice websites and books will recommend finding time to share as a couple, but in today's world, with both of you at full tilt, this can seem like Too Much Trouble. I have found that rather than arranging a long weekend, or hitting a nightclub dressed in bondage gear until 3 a.m., the small snatched hours or moments can really work. The arrangement to meet for coffee or lunch in town, or a quick bite when the kids are at a birthday party, or even popping baby in to Granny's for an hour whilst you both have a walk or do something less ambitious can be good. There will come a time when you will be able to climb the south face of the Eiger together if that's what you both want, and sooner than you think. And sometimes not just time together but time apart

can help, a chat with a friend, a game of squash, a party with the old rugby club from which we return bright-eyed and with that all-important commodity – news.

Chapter Five

This Isn't the Way My Life Was Supposed to Turn Out: Home vs. Work and Who Makes the Rules?

'Organisers helped at Agricultural Shows throughout the country. Mrs Frawley attended a Rural Week . . . in Roscrea (where the North Tipperary Federation had staged a fine display of handcrafts) and gave demonstrations; Ann Roche organised Poultry and Gardening Tests in Co. Cork and attended the Beekeepers' Conference in Sligo where she passed her Junior Beekeeper's Examination . . .'

Irish Countrywomens Association,
Progress Report since Council Meeting
in Cavan, July 1948

I met an acquaintance in the street the other day, as I was wheeling the bike home from school, listening to my three children whine, bicker and chatter. I have done this every day for the last four years, and sometimes feel as if I will be doing precisely this for ever. I will be found, aged eighty-five, pushing a bike up the Rathmines Road, and onlookers will 'tsk' sympathetically as I take my ghost children to school. 'That poor woman, she's been pushing that bike up the road for forty years now . . .'

My friend, a high-powered TV journalist, was tentatively pushing a pink buggy along the street, a look I recognized on her face, that mixture of bewilderment, terror and love that marks the first-time mother. 'I didn't know you'd had a baby,' I said, cooing at the cute nine-month-old inside the pram, chewing contentedly on his little fist, looking up at us with big brown eyes.

'Yes, little Aidan,' she smiled adoringly, before continuing in the same breath, 'but I am *working*, you know.' I haven't turned into some vegetable, like you, I could almost hear her say, as she eyed me and my three children warily, as if by coming into too-close contact with us, she might catch some disease. The contagion of stay-at-home motherhood to which she, unlike thousands of her sisters before her, would not succumb.

I was amused and mildly offended. That was me, I thought, ten years before, assuming that being a working mother was a simple act of will and that women who 'gave up' work to look after their children were basically wimps. You'll learn, I thought wryly, like some maternal sage, as she trotted off, Bugaboo pushed firmly ahead of her, to the life that she hadn't given up for her son.

Believe me, I can understand my friend's terror that this is all her life might be, from wheeling and dealing, to wheeling a buggy down to the shops, wondering if it'll be pasta or mince tonight: I was once that mother, determined to show that even though I had three children, I could still do everything that my education and class had designed me to do. Wanting to fulfil the hopes and dreams I had for myself as well as for my children. After all, unlike my mother and grandmother, I was lucky: I had a 'choice'.

*

In parenting, there is often one decision made about how you will raise your children, whether it be to provide them with the best education that you can, or to raise them in a particular religion, that defines your parenting life. In my case – and in my husband's – the 'choice' was that one of us would stay at home to look after the children. First, it was his turn and now it's mine. Like my father and grandfather, my husband now marches out the door every morning, briefcase in hand, into the big bad world of work and I, the little woman, stay at home, fill the dishwasher, make the beds, fetch and carry from school, take to the dentist, engage in the endless tasks of parenthood and in the simple pleasures too.

Yet, unlike my mother and grandmother, I *could* have done something else. I could have made the choice to work, waving my babies a cheery goodbye every morning as I left them in the care of Svetlana from Belarus; I could have been one of those mothers in the lifestyle supplements who have discovered the power of the Internet to market baby travel products, or hand-made smocks, or control pants which, it is implied, will be extra handy if you've let yourself go a bit. I, too, could utter the buzz phrases 'working around the children', 'flexibility' or the ghastly 'work–life balance'. I could have the best of both worlds, a fulfilling job *and* time at home with my family. What could be better?

*

But in fact, a lot of the current 'motherhood as lifestyle' stuff, the hand-knitted sling-making, the organic freezer-meal companies, the outsize maternity-bra mail-order concerns, reveals the stark reality of 'choice' for us mothers nowadays. The compromises, limitations, and that less trendy buzzword 'sacrifice' or, 'giving up' – there's not too much of that in the lifestyle supplements. Or the fact that perhaps rather than true change having taken place, the goalposts have simply moved, leaving us with the illusion of choice when the reality is entirely different.

What if, leaving aside the nice little part-time job, or the entrepreneurial sideline, it all boils down to leaving your career behind? 'Giving up' a career carries a whiff of martyrdom, that as a mother you have fallen on your sword, waving goodbye to a pension, to intellectual and social fulfilment and to an independent income, to push a buggy up and down the road to the shopping centre for the rest of your days. 'Choosing' to continue to work implies that you are headed for a life of stress, burnout and the inevitable neglect of your children as you 'put work first', i.e. are a bad mother.

Is the choice these days, in our world of endless choices, really that stark, children *or* job; to progress through the hard-won stages of your career, gritting your teeth as you try to reorganize your life because the nanny has walked out – again, having to apologize to your son because you can't watch him be the third goldfish on the right in his school play because you have a board meeting, wrestling with gut-wrenching feelings of guilt as your child misses out on playdates and lazy summer afternoons, asking yourself if you are simply putting your needs before your child's? Or to throw in the towel, to spend the next ten years in a damp playground, bored out of your mind in front of CBeebies, screaming at the kids to shut up for God's sake, idly wondering what you can stick in the oven for dinner and if half-five is too early to lash into the red wine?

These are questions I've had time to ponder over the last ten years. I have worked full-time, part-time, flexibly, you name it, trying to hang onto some vestige of my own identity *and* spend time with my children. I have 'given up' a promising career to hang around the aforementioned damp playgrounds, and in the process have become a person I never thought I would. I have gained peace and tranquillity and the pleasure of seeing my children grow, and I have lost something of myself, the vital, lively, engaged person I once was. For me, this 'choice' has played out in many ways, but it has certainly not been straightforward.

*

Of course, being able to do what you like with your life is a new idea, unique really to our generation. Nana never did what she wanted with her life: her adored father died when she was a teenager, and a life of genteel poverty ensued, where a veneer of good manners and a smart coat concealed the threadbare clothes and rumbling stomach underneath. Nana's two older brothers married immediately, and so Nana was promptly whipped out of Holy Faith Convent School in Clarendon Street and her happy life of Irish dancing and piano-playing and packed off to Cassidy's clothes shop, to support the family by advising the matrons of Dublin on skirt sizes and stocking types. Nana wanted to be an Irish dancing teacher, and always felt the loss of her ambitions keenly, speaking about them wistfully in later years, as well as the burden of responsibility for her not-entirely-driven siblings, whom my mother dismisses as 'not up to much', a warm-hearted bunch, full of fun and devilment, and given to much piano-playing and general jollity, if not much in the way of pulling themselves up by the bootstraps.

So, when Nana met my granddad and he began to appear in Cassidy's at the end of her shift, it must have seemed like a passport to another life, away from the responsibilities of her large, dependent family and into a comfortable middle-class life of golf, fishing, flower arranging and foreign holidays in the cleansing air of the Alps. They moved to Arklow, but once my mother started to grow, Nana wanted to do more with her life than polish the silver. She wanted to open her own business, a clothes shop, which would have suited her down to the ground, given her passion for fashion and outgoing – if offbeat – personality, but Granddad refused on the grounds that Nana's role purveying blouses to the good ladies of Arklow would reflect badly on his own as a servant of the state, assessing people's eligibility for social welfare benefits.

Once again, Nana's ambitions were thwarted. She

deferred to Granddad, as she did in everything; he was a very considerate husband for his time, my mother tells me, in that he didn't beat her up and disappear to the pub for hours on end; he gave her adequate amounts of housekeeping money and encouraged her to pursue her interests outside the home – as long as they didn't conflict with his own, it would seem. Nana accepted his decision stoically, as deferring to Jack was more important than fulfilling her own interests. She accepted that, when it came to working, she was not in control of her own destiny. For Nana, there was no such thing as choice.

Forty years later, my mother's ambitions would be thwarted by the infamous 'marriage bar', the expression of conservative Ireland's desire to keep mothers out of work and at home where they should be, making big dinners, doing a bit of Irish dancing and knitting Aran sweaters.[9] When I was little, I used to love digging out my mother's old photos of her time in Aer Lingus, about which she spoke as if it was the most excitement she'd ever had in her entire life, the implication clearly being

9. In *Women and Work in Ireland* (Economic and Social History Society of Ireland, 1999), Mary E. Daly states that 'attitudes in the Irish Free State were extremely hostile to the employment of women, particularly married women outside the home . . . The new state imposed a succession of discriminatory measures against working women. From the early 1920s women civil servants were forced to resign on marriage; in 1934 the marriage ban was extended to all national school teachers . . . this hostile climate culminated in article 41.2 of the 1937 Constitution, which emphasised a woman's place within the home.'

that she wasn't having half as much fun now. There were glamorous black-and-white shots of my mother and her fellow airline staff in their Jackie Kennedy uniforms, standing with a smiling pilot around a model DC9. Faces full of life and fun, reflecting the glamour and excitement of air travel, particularly to the Mecca that was America in the 1950s, a watershed for my mother, awestruck by the huge cars, fridges, tons of food and bright clothes at a time when Ireland could not have been more impoverished, grey and repressive.

Even though my mother protests that she was happy to embrace domestic life as her destiny, when I was younger and embarking on my own career, she frequently talked about how she had had 'no choice' but to leave Aer Lingus, as women weren't allowed to stay on once they got married, and if they attempted to flout the bar, they were demoted, as her best friend found out when she returned briefly after marriage. Instead, Mum moved in with Dad, into his family home in the suburbs, taking on Dad's elderly, deaf and eccentric grandfather in the process, along with a menagerie of his friends and an elderly gardener whom he had adopted years before and who now lived in a shed in the back garden, shouting and roaring at all hours of the day and night. There she brought up her three children, knitting her way through the days, working her way through the oeuvre of Fanny Cradock and trying to stop my brother from strangling the next-door neighbour's baby or poisoning the school goldfish, which he proudly did one day by feeding them talcum powder.

My mother's choices were limited either to embracing the domestic arena, or to find other, socially acceptable ways of earning money such as taking in lodgers or Spanish students. We had a former clerical student who used to give me lifts to the shop on his Honda 50, which I thought was terrifyingly exciting; he also kept a stash of mint Club Milks in his sock drawer which my friend and I would try to steal when he was out at lectures. We also invited a succession of bewildered middle-aged Japanese people to stay every summer for a couple of weeks, courtesy of some gig Mum had going with a local tour entrepreneur. But, in spite of eating a lot of tempura, and some interesting cultural exchanges, I suspect this isn't what my mother wanted. Her frustration at the narrowness of her horizons was palpable when I was small – it pervaded every corner of our suburban home, from the pointed click-clack of her knitting needles to the scrape, scrape of the trowel in the flower beds.

*

Unlike my mother and grandmother, who were expected to stay at home with their families after the requisite six months spent working at something harmless, I chose to stay at home because I *had* the choice. After all, I wanted to do 'something else', to embark on a new and interesting career. But I'm not sure it's really as simple as that, or if I and my fellow mothers have really attained that nirvana of working motherhood that we were brought up to expect. Before I had my children, I had assumed that I would continue doing what I had been doing before I had them, only with them, if you see what I mean. Neatly packaged away with a minder, I would return to the office and smile fondly at photos of them on my desk, or take interesting phone calls from them as I wielded my pen over another author's work. At the same time, I would attain perfection as an exemplary mother, devoted to my children. I was caught up in the twenty-first-century myth that we can be perfect mothers and mistresses of our own destiny.

My mother once wistfully remarked, 'You are such a conscientious mother, you know, I was just . . . so . . . distracted.' Quite apart from the fact that I don't, as she did, have an autistic child to look after with little support, I think that conscientious is the right word – dutiful, trying to ensure that only the very best will suffice. One of the key things for me, which has influenced all of my decisions about working as a mother, is that I wanted to get it 'right' somehow. Unlike my mother and my grandmother, who of course wanted to be good mothers but who didn't treat it like a PhD thesis, I wanted to focus on my children in a 'proper' way, to steer them through their childhood and to be a reasonably steady presence. I wanted to have 'quality' time with them – I wasn't going to leave them to roam unsupervised for the day whilst I hoovered and polished, telling them to disappear and not to come back until dinner time. I was going to be there, being positive and encouraging, not like mothers in my own generation, who had dished out the kind of lacerating criticism that would prevent us getting above ourselves. But I also wanted to maintain my own identity and hard-won career. Which should be possible in this day and age, shouldn't it?

*

I began my search for parental perfection, and my life as a working mother, when my eldest was a baby and we had returned home from London to the aforementioned seaside town. Still in the throes of first-time motherhood, my project, to be the Best Mother in the Entire World, was going well. My poor eldest son was the focus of my entire being, as I poured heart and soul into bringing him up. I would spend hours devising nutritious meals for him, and pondering what snacks would provide maximum nutritional benefit – he was very keen on popcorn, until a friend told me that it contained enough salt to shut down his kidneys, whereupon I indulged in much hand-wringing and monitoring him for any signs of kidney failure. I spent hours entertaining the poor child, selecting just the right kind of music for him to listen to, carefully ignoring the fact that whether I put on Elvis or Mozart he was entirely indifferent; or walking along the beach with him showing him the stones and bits of seaweed to provide him with the kind of early-years education that would result in him being a genius. I pushed the buggy up to parenting classes, given by two firm-busted middle-aged ladies with hair that resembled candy floss, who told me that even to mention the world 'bold' to my child – the Irish term for 'naughty' – would scar him for life. I diligently noted recipes for Play-Doh and had a go at making cotton-wool sheep.

So used was I to 'focus' and 'goals' and 'scheduling' in my life that I applied the same – unnecessary – manic zeal to motherhood, anxious not to repeat what I saw as the mistakes and the ignorance of previous generations. I was far more sophisticated than my mother and grandmother, I thought to myself. What I didn't want to admit was that I felt entirely marooned in my new life. I longed to be able to walk to the shops – a distance of about half a mile – in the allotted fifteen minutes, and not in an hour, examining every bit of dog poo on the way. I found the structureless time with tiny tots, the constant sense that the afternoon stretched ahead of you, without the markers of homework, dinner and playdate that comes with older children, along with conversation and fun, hard to cope with. The only thing that saved me was the mother-and-toddler group, held in the local Baptist church, where we mothers would sit under cheerful pictures of Jesus shepherding a multicultural group of children, eating chocolate biscuits and sharing our little stories of colic and night-feeding and the sheer lonely grind of early-years motherhood.

In order to give my children my undivided attention and to maximize their early-years potential, I had chosen not to look for a job in an office, but instead spent a couple of years freelancing. This would, I thought, give me the best of both worlds, allowing me to flex my intellectual muscles *and* to be übermom. I ended up editing a social science journal, trying to cajole brief pieces on relative poverty out of social scientists who weren't exactly go-getters. 'I think it's important that everyone be on board the ship before it leaves for shore, rather than just the captain,' one of them said sniffily when I enquired when he might be thinking of producing his piece on housing inequality in the Euro Zone. After ten years working with lovely lady novelists with big hair and bigger storylines, or macho thriller writers who may or may not have been in the SAS, weedy, angst-ridden people moaning about how terrible it was that poor people were, like, *poor*, tried my patience. More importantly, I found it hard to adjust to my diminished status as a freelancer. My choice to 'get it right' had led me into a life of boredom and frustration and – a recurring theme for us working mothers – low status: I began to feel uncomfortably like my mother.

When writing about this a memory returned to me of the shop-bought mini pizzas Mum instructed me to 'cook' for my brother and young sister when she was out at work. I was ten years old, and with Ireland in the depths of a recession my mother had found herself a 'little job' to help pay the bills. A gang of her lady friends, all of whom were in more or less the same boat of middle-class straightened circumstances, shared a few hours working at a local launderette run by a friend of theirs, a back-up to her husband's irregular job in the theatre. Several mornings a week, between 10 a.m. and 2 p.m., my mother would repair to the whirring machines and warm fuggy air, to the bag washes and chat on an upturned laundry basket at break-times, to the boss, who would break each morning at 10.30 with, 'Fancy sharing a Kit-Kat?', a hopeful look in his eyes meaning that you had to say yes, what could be nicer? The little town in which she worked had a transient population and a substantial heroin problem at the time and so every wisp of human life would drift in her door, requesting an extra wash to remove the bloodstains from their clothing, issuing physical threats if their washing wasn't done on time.

My mother's job was referred to by Dad as for 'pin money', a 'few bob', as were all women's jobs at the time, the understanding being that low-status jobs were all that these relatively well-educated women could aspire to. Something non-threatening, that wouldn't essentially change their status as stay-at-home mothers and the centre of their families' lives. But I could at least aspire to something better. When I was offered my fiction job, I had something to prove, after three years of inadequate parenting in which I hadn't lived up to my own expectations that it would all be lovely and I would be a natural, discovering a hitherto ignored passion for domestic life. And mothering hadn't lived up to my expectations either, that it would be a fluffy-wuffy powder puff of love, with no crying, shouting or mess, and that my children would think I was the most wonderful mother (they did anyway, which acceptance always astounds me and which should be of some comfort to us mothers).

I had no qualms about leaving my children in the tender care of my husband for the simple reason that he was much, much better at the job than I – and he seemed to like it, or if he didn't, I didn't ask. Maybe I could be good at work, even if I wasn't a Real Mother, I thought to myself, embracing it with the enthusiasm of someone who was happy to be back, basking in the glow of rediscovering this part of myself: joining in every boring office conversation about home furnishing, about whether or not dogs could be left at home all day, where the best place to get sun-dried tomatoes was, or discussing the plotlines of *Desperate Housewives*. After three years in the wilderness, I was, finally, somebody, with Important Stuff to Do. My days revolved around marketing and editorial meetings, author lunches and launches and being an all-round editorial sage and guru. And it was fun. Motherhood had given me the confidence to at least pretend well. I was no longer the quaking desk editor in London, pencil poised over some work of science fiction, afraid to ask my boss what Cyber-punk was. Suddenly, I was a real editor.

What's more, my status took a stratospheric leap upwards. I was no longer a pair of hands attached to a buggy, a harassed mum in a scraggy pony tail with a wailing baby at the checkout, but a Working Mother and, what's more, the last word in editing savvy. My authors – well, most of them – seemed to appreciate my words of wisdom and my keen eye on their work. 'What do you think, Alison?' was a question that constantly surprised me – that people were asking for my opinion on something was vaguely thrilling.

Just as I had envisioned all those years ago, at my desk with its little plastic tidy and pinboard, I displayed photographs of my children, occasionally looking up from my work at the photo of my eldest laughing beside his impressive Lego tower, or my daughter standing on a chair, aged eighteen months, 'talking' into the telephone. My children were suddenly disembodied, no longer um-bilically attached to me, their sticky little hands twisting my skirt around as they stood behind me in the shop, or sitting on my knee, reading a story, as my son used to do, hand placed around my neck, eyes taking in every word of *Noddy Goes to Toytown*.

I thrived as the Woman Who Could Do Everything. I didn't honestly miss my children during the day, the cutting and sticking, the little naps, the cheese-or-tuna-sandwich-for-lunch; I enjoyed my work, even though boredom was replaced by a certain glassy-eyed dementia, there suddenly never being enough hours in the day, when once there were too many. From being an endless vista of small tasks to fill the time, the day became a busy whirlwind of scheduled activity. What fun. But then the focus shifted. The job, when it built up into something, was all-consuming – I seemed to have gone from one extreme to the other; from counting the hours until bedtime to frantically trying to fit my entire life into one tiny day; from stay-at-home mum of foosthering[10] over a wooden jigsaw or a batch of fairy cakes to Man About the House, stomping in of an evening and throwing my carrier bags full of manuscripts down, sighing gustily as I reached for the remote control. And then my youngest son was born and the careful equilibrium of my life shifted subtly, but inexorably, towards something else.

At the zenith of my 'how does she do it all' phase, I also wrote a weekly column for a newspaper, detailing in light-hearted, self-deprecating fashion the trials and tribulations of my life as a working mother of two, and then three. Based on one of these columns, I was asked to go on a radio show and talk about my essential superhumanity: 'How do you do it all, Alison,' the interviewer asked me, 'the job, the column, the children, I mean, really, you have it all, don't you?'

10. 'Foosthering', i.e. fussing pointlessly, is one of those descriptive Irish words like 'eejit', the English equivalent of which seems pale by comparison.

Well, there's the thing Jimmy, I thought to myself as I wittered on about how terrific online shopping was: I feel burnt-out, exhausted from trying to pretend to kick ass when all I want to do is lie under my desk and have a little sleep, I haven't spoken to my husband in weeks because we are too busy/tired and stressed, and are both convinced that the other is in nirvana whilst we are toiling away at the coalface. I have spent half my maternity leave editing next season's books because apparently I am the only person who could do it, in a job that looks as if it is experimental to say the least. I haven't slept in a year because my youngest spends twenty-three hours out of twenty-four crying. But really, it's fantastic!

When I had my third child, the working-mother phase in my life seemed to come to an abrupt end, like a train hitting the buffers. I discovered that working and being a mother at the same time is hard going: it's not just the constant splitting of yourself between work and home, but the keeping up of appearances on both fronts — that I could be a busy professional person who just had to dash out of the production meeting to listen to my eldest proclaim the line, 'I see a light!' at his school Christmas play; that I couldn't bang on about my children all the time for fear of being seen as some airhead who couldn't work out what her priorities are; and more pressingly, that I could still Be A Good Mother.

Ah, yes, that was the killer. I didn't want to be the mother who let her child down by being the only one to produce shop-bought cake for the school bake sale, thus branding him/her with the mark of Cain – 'Poor Alison doesn't have the time to make a coffee sponge,' the ladies on the parents' committee would sigh, meaning, 'Alison is a neglectful mother who doesn't have her priorities right and her child will suffer as a consequence.' I would thus break my neck to get home from my office in an industrial estate in the arse end of nowhere, to school to attend the Daffodil Day bake sale, clutching a lukewarm cup of tea in my hand, manically grinning whilst trying to remember if I'd typed that offer letter to the literary agent. I would screech in late to my daughter's ballet recital, dropping bits of paper, mobile phone tweeting, and would also rush in late to every marketing meeting, sitting down in my seat before realizing I was sitting on some unpleasantly sticky something that one of my children had left on my skirt. It seemed as if I was caught between two worlds, pulled inexorably back and forth.

I'd loved my job: the fun, stimulation and enjoyment of being good at something, but after the birth of my youngest son, my perspective radically shifted. Everything that I had wanted seemed suddenly less important: I had reached a new phase in my life where the sacred rituals of the office no longer seemed as appealing; when I contemplated looking out the office window at the canal from now until the day I retired and thought, 'No, that's not what I want.' Could there be another life out there for me?

And I couldn't leave my son behind with his lovely minder every day without feeling every single minute of it. He was six months old, and I would leave every morning, head full of sleep, trying to pull my brain together to face a day of tough, task-oriented decision-making, when all I wanted was to sit on the sofa with him and play clap-hands, to grasp the rolls of wobbly fat around his middle, to see whether he preferred stewed apple or carrot, to trot along to the shops to buy lunch, to have peace and space and time, all of the things that I had abandoned with enthusiasm five years before.

I reached my decision in London, after my first visit to head office since my son's birth. I had cycled into town that morning, briefcase on my back carrier, racing down the canal to catch the 6.30 a.m. airport bus, winter wind streaming past my ears, thinking, I don't want to be going to London, I want to be at home, looking out the window at the trees, baby banging his spoon on his highchair table. I stumbled onto the plane and looked out of the window, trying to gather my thoughts together into some form of coherence to face my first editorial meeting in a year. Instead, I blubbed all the way to London, snuffling into my damp tissue on the Heathrow Express to Paddington. I managed to hold my shit together for the editorial meeting, at which I was to be a guest, smiling at my colleagues, who warmly welcomed me back from maternity leave, listening with some interest to the discussions about cover approaches and editing deadlines, suppressing the urge to hurl myself onto the boardroom table and sob loudly. Quite frankly, I wasn't in my right mind, but a blubbing, leaking mess who was still umbilically attached to her baby. I managed to get to my hotel, a bleak place in Knightsbridge that smelt vaguely of drains, where I spent a restless night watching TV programmes about Colombian drugs cartels, there being nothing else on at 3 a.m., and dragged myself out of bed the next morning to get to a meeting at a trendy eatery with an agent. In the whole of my health I would have loved this gossipy, glamorous place, and the opportunity to spot several celebrities, but instead I chewed on my muesli, only pretending to listen to the agent chattering on about the author's brave new direction, nodding my head and uhming when I thought it was required. And then suddenly I thought, 'That's it, I'm out of here.' I changed my flight, got on the Tube and went home. A month later, I handed in my notice. Another choice was made.

*

I can see that the aforementioned looks like Middle-Class Moaning, as I call it; whining vaguely about whatever situation you happen to be in, that it's not *quite* perfect enough, that there is something missing: motherhood isn't absolutely perfect, cue the therapist; working with children is hard too, so we moan about that.

And, yes, I do think that there is something of the Stepford in our approach to modern Mum-dom, making us put vast amounts of pressure on ourselves. Of this, I am a living example. And, unlike thousands of mothers, I made a choice out of my own free will. I was in a position where I could envisage taking a break without the bailiffs coming in to repossess – well, not immediately. I read about mothers who have had no choice but to work, stoically slogging through their children's lives because they alone are responsible for their upbringing – and managing just fine, without any of the hand-wringing that has accompanied my efforts – and I feel a start of guilt at my weepy failure to tough it out. What a smack in the mouth to my mother's generation, slogging in the launderette and 'making do' with a variety of little jobs, putting their hopes and dreams for themselves on hold to ensure that their daughters got the opportunities of which they'd been deprived.

But the fact of the matter is, the choice to stay at home is easier than the choice to work. With my husband now working full-time, it was easier for me to throw in the towel than to find a nice lady to mind the children, to organize a car-pool rota that resembles the military plans for the assault on El-Alamein, not to forget the weekly online shop, or the dentists' visits, or enduring the critical looks of other mothers who felt that my children were neglected – so I simply gave up the struggle.

Another irony of our lives as working mothers these days is that in some ways it is harder to work than it was for our grandmothers. If Nana had got her wish to open a shop, she, like every other middle-class woman at the time, would simply have got a maid, a nice country girl who would have polished all day long and burned the dinner. At one stage, my mother had a lodger called Bridget, a young girl who came to stay in the 'study', which had been Dad's grandfather's room before he died, one of a succession of guests whom my mother took in to make ends meet. A student teacher, she took a great interest in Ian, teaching him to read at the age of three, and for a year or two my mother had the support she needed to allow her to dream of other things, but it was tantalizingly short-lived. Bridget moved on after college and my mother got on with life as usual. And, although I had to press my mother to admit it, she did acknowledge that, yes, she would have liked to do 'something', a little bit sooner than the speech and drama qualification she got when we were 'well reared' as we say here, i.e. in our twenties.

Nowadays, I can't afford the kind of help that would allow me to work full-time, even if I wanted to, nor do I have a granny handy, with nothing else to do but look after my children. Unlike Nana, who would live a full thirty years longer than her husband and who had lots of time to devote to her only child and her family, my mother has the life-long responsibility of my brother to keep her occupied, so to ask her for more seems churlish. And so, the 'choice' is to work, with less support than ever before.

I could have worked part-time for a while, as my employer was happy to let me do so. So why not – how many working mothers would give their eye teeth for a flexible employer? Unlike my mother and grandmother, people were actually *asking* me to work, delighted that I had come back after my third child and thrusting spreadsheets in front of me, which I looked at as if they were in Hebrew. My employer assumed that I had returned to work the same person as when I had left – cheerful, energetic – not this weepy, burnt-out wreck, and put all sorts of new adventurous ideas to me about where my list could go next, but I had been on the rollercoaster for four years and had nothing left in the tank to give to cookery books or true crime, or to the frantic routine of work/home/ironing/shopping. I didn't have the nerve to say to my boss that I just wasn't able to work at full throttle right now (or possibly ever), and so I stumbled on, until I felt that I had no option but to 'give up'.

I am well aware that, to some women, I might be a living example of the rationale some employers use to get rid of women who return to work after maternity leave: 'a bit the worse for wear', too 'emotional' to deal with the cut and thrust of the marketing meeting. But the truth of it is, motherhood is as much personal as political. Perhaps I should have held on grimly by my fingernails, expressing milk in the loos and trying not to let my mind wander in meetings, in order not to let the sisterhood down, but I felt it was simply not for me. And yes, it's a selfish choice too, leaving most of the financial responsibility to my husband so that I could get off the treadmill at a time when money was in short supply.

*

I know that over the last ten years of being a mother I have made choices about how to work, about where and when to use my skills, or about whether to work at all for a while. But whilst, of course, I am responsible for all of my decisions, I'm not sure if these were 'choices' in a real sense: sure, I decided to accept the department store voucher instead of a twenty-hour week, but the fact is, the choices I made were within a limited framework, and I expect I'm not alone.

I'm not suggesting that things haven't improved since my mother's and grandmother's day: there is a general cultural acceptance that women work: the days of the shoulder-padded superwoman returning to the office three hours after giving birth, because if she didn't, she'd be seen as a wimp, are over, and men don't get away with dismissing their partner's desire to work in the way that my granddad dismissed his wife's, but in a way the arguments are rather more insidious now; they have gone underground. Every so often some rich businessman will stick his head above the parapet and say out loud what every right-thinking *Daily Mail* reader already knows: that once a woman has a child, her work will become 'less important' to her: or even if he doesn't say it, he will act accordingly.

But is it simply too painful to admit that we haven't really come that far in the struggle for equality; that instead of real change, the goalposts have simply moved? That in some ways it is harder, rather than easier, for mothers to work now than it would have been in Victorian times? That 'choice' is just an invention of the time we live in, when we feel we should have everything, when we are raised to expect the world, and that compromise is for wimps?

*

A friend said to me the other day, 'You know, you made a big sacrifice for your children, giving up your career.' I'm not sure that, until then, I had really seen it that way. After all, I was forty, had three children, had worked at the same job for almost twenty years, and I felt like a jaded old hag, cigarette in my hand, blowing smoke over the dreams of tender young writers. I felt as if I'd seen everything before, every possible variation on the Mr Right novel, I was cynical and burnt out, feeling the need to press the pause button just for a while. And here I am, pushing the bike to school and back, occupying the netherworld, as my TV friend might see it, of 'flexible work', a little bit of writing here, a touch of editing there, which allows me to spend time with my children whilst continuing to engage, on some level, with the working world and with the difficult business of earning a living.

I didn't intend to continue to edit: I had plans, big plans. But somehow these have got slightly derailed under a pile of damp underwear and peanut-butter sandwiches and the endless bills that I now realize need to be paid, not shoved into the drawer under the microwave. I wanted to be someone, and yet here I am, doing what I always have done, but for less money, accorded less respect and having to pay my own overheads.

I haven't found myself at all, but instead have, in spite of myself, been a stay-at-home mother in the true sense of the word. In the sandwich-making, swimming-togs-washing, after-school-ferrying, playdate-supervising sense of the word, that is. This isn't what I wanted, but now that I have it, I find it a surprising revelation. And no, I'm not about to launch into one of those ghastly diatribes about the joys of Being at Home for My Children, implying that anyone who isn't, isn't a 'real mother', before I go off to knit a few jumpers, bake the bread for their sandwiches myself, polish the brasses and make my husband a three-course meal before engaging in a night's tantric sex, but I've been surprised by how I have managed to adapt to my new life and make something of it. The kind of relative success that, deep down, I felt I never made with my working life, in spite of all the *Sturm und Drang*.

Instead of being a lonely planet orbiting quietly around my baby, feeling that I and he/she were the only people in the world, I am part of a pleasant, sociable solar system of mothers at the school gate, or at the swimming pool, or in the local café. And the quiet routine – of school, home, school, park, homework, TV, play, dinner, bed – comes as something of a relief after the grind of working life. There's nobody breathing down my neck any more about sales figures, no guilt-filled examination of the bestseller lists knowing that one of my authors will be on the phone to me next week, wondering why they're not on it. And, in spite of feeling distinctly murderous several times a day, I enjoy my children more, their jokes and their perspective on the world, being told 101 things I didn't know about nits or space travel, seeing them enjoy things and enjoying their successes, being as thrilled if they win the weekly medal for the best effort in Irish speaking as if I had won it myself.

The important thing I have learned from being at home with my children *and* being a working mother is that the concept of choice is a complex one. The moral of the story is that nothing really works when you have growing children. No solution is ideal and somehow we have to just get through it, until we reach the high plateau of adolescence when we will have lots of time to develop ourselves once more, time to attend the University of the Third Age, whilst trying to ignore the fact that our children are running riot all over the place with bottles of cider in their hands. And, whilst we ought not to accept that restricted choices should be conferred upon us – the polite enquiries as to whether we'll be downscaling now that we are having a baby, making room for someone of the male persuasion who will never be going on maternity leave, or that the most we can expect is a little part-time job in the charity shop because people think we are capable of nothing – we have perhaps to accept the uncomfortable truth that parenthood involves compromise. That our choices might be limited for a time; that having it all has become a stick to beat ourselves with. Of course, I want a fulfilling job, lots of money *and* time with my kids, but I've had to choose. And for the moment, I am trying to accept my choices with Zen-like stoicism, that for the time being this is as perfect as it gets.

Take It from Me

* Try not to judge the decisions your fellow mothers make. So what if Deirdre wants to leave little Sebastian in the care of a plastic-coated, lank-haired, miserable girl from the outer reaches of Europe because she's got a board meeting? This does not make her a Bad Mother, just a mother who needs to get away from her children for a bit. Equally, you might pity poor stay-at-home Eva, constantly filling

her time with little trips to the supermarket, or hand-knitting egg cosies for the school fair, because she has 'nothing better to do', but Eva is happy, believe it or not, and her children are, too.

* Do not spend your time at home with pursed lips and a martyred look on your face, banging on at your children about all the much more exciting things you could be doing with your life: they didn't ask you to give up your 200K-a-year job as a City trader to sit at home making brownies.

* A lot of mothers have spoken to me about the dangers of expressing yourself through your children: about becoming the scourge of the parents' committee, manically organizing every fundraiser and hanging around the schoolyard with a scary look on your face. Similarly, you will not find fulfilment by pushing your children through four years of Suzuki, or sticking a hurley in your son's hand, when that son has hopeless hand-eye coordination. You won't find it by arranging birthday parties for your children which are so elaborate that the emperor Nero would have benefitted from your organizational tips. We all need to hang on to something that is ours, whether it be macramé or our passion for Acid House, that is a child-free zone and that makes us feel good about ourselves, not about little Derek.

* Which brings me to perfection. It is simply not attainable; I should know – I've tried, spending all my time reproaching myself for everything I have done wrong as a mother; examining every barked comment, every sharp aside to my children, weighing up just how much psychological damage it'll be doing them; striving for perfection in sandwich-making, costume-sewing, parental attendance at boring dance recitals. Perfection becomes another stick to beat yourself with, and life is hard enough.

* No matter what you decide, whether to work or to stay at home, to knit fair-isle jumpers until 2 a.m. to bring the money in, or to sit on the train for two hours commuting to the office because you don't want to give up your job, try to avoid my own particular bête noir: guilt. Guilt about not being at home, guilt about not being at work, guilt about neglecting your partner, guilt about asking your mother to babysit for the fifteenth time, etc. . . . it's draining and benefits no one, least of all you. Trust me, I have a degree in guilt.

* Don't get caught up in the casual office remarks that diminish mothers: about how brain-dead Fran is since she came back from maternity leave, or how disgusting it was that she breastfed Jimmy in the production meeting, or, gosh, is she out again because

Jimmy's teething? People have all kinds of responsibilities even if they don't have children: elderly mothers, demented aunties, cats who need taking to the vet. People have lives, and when you need to take a morning off to go to the dentist, Fran will hopefully be nicer to you than you were to her.

Chapter Six

'A Lovely Bit of Bacon': Getting in Touch with My Inner Housewife

'At the monthly meeting there is usually a talk with some such title as "autumn work in the garden" . . . "highlights of our local history", "how to keep well in winter". There might also be a demonstration of some practical value to countrywomen in dealing with their work in the home and around the farm. Handcrafts are encouraged primarily as a help to beautify the home . . . cookery, cheese-making, embroidery, rug-making . . .'

Irish Countrywomens Association
claim to a bequest from the late
Charlotte Shaw, January 1952

In the months after I finished work, I developed a curious mania for housework, lifting the sofa to hoover out the dust from underneath, removing all of the sofa covers every week and sending them to the grumpy Polish man in the dry cleaners; grimly driving bags full of recycling to the recycling centre; scrubbing the bathroom tiles with a nailbrush to reveal the colour they had once been, and not just the coating of grime which had formed a fine patina over the blue mosaic. Perhaps a little bit of me thought that cleaning and mopping could fill the vacuum left by work, that spraying the front doorstep with Dettol at every opportunity would help me to forget that once I used to do something else. I had practically sprinted out of the office, such was my eagerness to depart, but once I'd had my little holiday and bade the childminder farewell, taking my lovely bald little baby back into my arms, I was unanchored in my new life; I tickled him under the chin as he gurgled with laughter, inhaling the soft fuzzy smell at the top of his head, the damp curls sticking to his forehead. I am where I should be, I thought, as I watched him crawl around the kitchen, picking up a shrivelled pea from underneath the table between thumb and forefinger, or quietly emptying the laundry basket, or smearing his sister's Bratz strawberry-flavoured lip gloss all over his mouth as he bounced solemnly up and down to her Scissor Sisters CD.

But who am I now? This would take me some time to work out, to settle into the life I had now chosen, and even longer to create a new one. But in the meantime, I had chosen to stay at home and I could hardly eschew a perfectly good salary to lie around watching cookery programmes and eating chocolate biscuits. To justify my new, brave and rather self-centred decision, I had to look busy.

And so, for the next few months, I threw myself into my new domestic role, practically assaulting my vaguely bewildered family with a range of awful dinners, singed lamb chops, so overcooked they would form a heap of ashes on the plate (as a vegetarian it has taken me some years to learn that meat is not a festering swamp of germs that have to be beaten into submission), overcooked pasta and lumpy mashed potato. Until then, my husband had done most of the cooking and my children's mournful glances at chicken with potato-crisp coating and lentil burgers with yoghurt dressing and other curiosities led me to understand that they still wished he did. My attempts at cleaning were equally wonky, with a number of appliances biting the dust during my tenure, including our beloved brown microwave – which we'd had for fifteen years – being flooded when I attacked it too enthusiastically with soap and water. The fury with which I attacked domestic life was palpable, the enthusiasm with which I would try to get various things to bend to my will, the perfectionist pursuit of a domestic nirvana which, believe me, didn't come naturally. It wasn't good enough just to do the jobs – they had to be done perfectly, but the harder I tried, the worse I got.

*

I didn't realize that in my strenuous housekeeping, I was unconsciously echoing my mother's and grandmother's daily struggles, the small rituals that made up their lives during a time when 'housekeeping' was becoming a job in itself, a desirable and respectable one and not just a necessity to keep germs and disease at bay whilst the myriad tasks of rural life were attended to – the feeding of livestock, the making of bread and dinners, the helping out in the fields – which formed a part of every Irish rural woman's life and which relegated 'housework' to a modest amount of cleaning and the drudgery of the Monday wash. The irony was that as electricity and running water came to the Irish countryside in the 1950s, so did a new 'job', that of housewife, with a new emphasis on sparkling tableware, clean surfaces and the mastery of the domestic routine which would previously have been considered a wild indulgence.[11] In the grim 1940s, with the privations of the Emergency in full swing, Nana was prepared to cook and clean for her husband and daughter, but a thick layer of dust was considered perfectly acceptable in her damp and elderly rented house – it could hardly be seen anyway under the dim, flickering electrical light bulbs. The goal didn't seem to have been to maintain a meticulously tidy house, but to keep the dust and dirt at a reasonable distance. The beds would be 'aired' every morning before being made, the top sheet folded carefully over the scratchy woollen blankets, and then 'dressed' in a chocolate brown bedspread, matching eiderdown and pillows. In the morning the dodgy Hoover would be dragged out and examined to see if it was working well enough to make any difference to the living-room carpet, the kitchen floor would be mopped and the 'dinner' made. Jack would return at lunchtime for the main meal of the day, after which Nana would read the paper for a bit and then get ready to go into town to place her next day's food orders with the butcher and the grocer, who would deliver to the house daily. Then she might meet friends for a cup of tea and a chat, amongst other topics jealously discussing Maeve O'Brien and how she 'worked' in the family business, a regular topic of conversation,

11. Source: Caitriona Clear, *Women of the House*, Chapter 7, 'The Day's Work'.

echoing their own secret desires to do something else with their lives. Nana's situation was fairly typical of many middle-class town-dwelling women at the time, and in spite of a lack of many of the conveniences that make our lives so 'easy', like a proper vacuum cleaner and one of those newfangled washing machines, her life wasn't the one of drudgery and brow-mopping slavery that we might think.

For my mother's generation of middle-class women, though, 'housework' was what you did, and if you had any self-respect at all, you did it well. The glorification of housework had begun. Food and domestic life had totemic power, a symbol of status when little other was available, of the care, love and attention which a mother could lavish on her family, as well as of sheer necessity when cheap clothes weren't available and ready meals had yet to be invented. My mother made all of my clothes when I was a child, because clothes were expensive and generally horrible, and so I spent a lot of time being told to stand still whilst various bits of corduroy were measured and pinned on me; but also because making beautiful handmade clothes was the visible evidence of your prowess. My mother had trained at the Grafton Academy of Dressmaking and was an expert seamstress; Sunday Mass was where she displayed her skills in competition with other mothers in a kind of holy fashion show.

And here I am, thirty years later, flapping a duster around and dousing everything with Mr Muscle. The mangle that my mother used to squeeze water out of the contents of the twin-tub has been replaced by a tumble drier in my home, the carpet sweeper that used to rush over the brown carpet tiles in the living room with an asthmatic wheeze is now a shiny Dyson whooshing over wooden floorboards and the hand-knitted Aran cardigans over which my mother used to labour have become cheap and cheerful clothing made in the Philippines. And yet the feeding, clothing and caring for children propels us back into the domestic sphere in a way which is different to my mother's time, but strikingly similar in many unsettling ways. The setting of fires and making of three-course dinners which took up so much of her time have been replaced by the pressures of work, the ferrying of children, the shepherding and fussing and ensuring of optimum attainment, the preparation of quick but nutritious meals, the impossibly high standards of contemporary mothering and the lack of the domestic help that my mother and grandmother would have cheerfully, non-guiltily, enjoyed. In many ways things are the same, but different, if you see what I mean.

*

Nowhere is the changing face of domestic life more apparent than in the preparation of food, the ultimate symbol of a mother's love and care for her family, which absorbed so much of my mother's and grandmother's time and which has an entirely different meaning for me.

On a recent visit to London I was thrilled to find a copy of a glorious *Good Housekeeping* cookery book from the 1950s in a little bric-a-brac shop on Essex Road. Full of eye-searing 'colour' shots of cold salmon *en gelée* and pig's head surprise, as well as every conceivable kind of useful recipe, my children and I have consulted it many times, feasting our eyes on the intricate displays of piping and copious use of gelatine, ooh-ing and aah-ing over elaborate jelly moulds and fiendishly complicated birthday cakes. These concoctions must have taken hours, we sigh. Where did they find the time?

But we forget that meal preparation would have formed a large part of my mother's and grandmother's day, when a three-course meal was an expectation at 'dinner' time, one o'clock, with soup followed by meat and two veg and stewed apple and custard, then 'tea' at six, with slices of cold ham, fresh lettuce, hard-boiled eggs and scallions. And a supply of apple tarts and home-baked scones would have been a reasonable expectation for the hordes of visitors who descended regularly: Nana would have hosted various members of her family who travelled to Arklow from Dublin for 'a holiday' by the sea, and my mother would have fed and looked after Dad's Granddad and the English relatives who appeared regularly with great fanfare and who all expected to be fed and looked after.

On special occasions, food would also give women like my mother a chance to shine. I remember as a child of about seven watching my mother with fascination as she prepared for a dinner party. The fish man turned up in his van and a couple of large brown crabs – alive, of course – were deposited into a red bucket filled with water. They sat in the kitchen corner under a tea-towel and when I could pluck up the courage I would sneak over and gingerly lift it, afraid that one of them would lunge out at me, but instead they just click-clacked there quietly for the rest of the afternoon. It being the 1970s, crab terrine was a popular starter, as was another of my mother's favourites, lamb's hearts, which I remember her stuffing with a mixture of parsley and breadcrumbs, or chicken-liver pâté, for which she confidently piled the purple, slimy chicken livers into the liquidizer along with a slab of butter, herbs and a glug of sherry. For dessert she would make a choux pastry ring, an elaborate confection filled with crème pâtissière, sprinkled with almonds and dusted with icing sugar, or an ice-cream 'bombe', an elaborate layering of sponge cake and ice-cream that would take her most of the afternoon to prepare. The whole idea of the dinner party was to wow your guests with the efforts to which you had gone to impress them, not, as do I, to casually throw together a bowl of pasta and a salad. By watching her, I was getting a glimpse into the private world of the adult, the rituals of the dinner party, the clinking glasses and murmured conversation punctuated by gusts of laughter, which I would listen to in my bed upstairs.

In our undemonstrative world, food was also a symbol of love: my mother didn't examine my paintings and school scribblings and exclaim loudly over their genius, instead she silently placed a home-made Danish pastry in front of me when I got home from school, or a ginger-bread man, or a still-warm apple sponge slice. Food and the rituals around it were at once a yoke around my mother's neck and something in which she found a peculiar kind of solace, along with the seasonal rituals of domestic life. January always meant marmalade-making, with a big tin of marmalade mix and dozens of tooth-achingly sour Seville oranges bubbling away in a huge pot on the cooker, to be poured when ready into the scalded glass jars lined up on the counter; in February, we seemed to exist on a diet of rhubarb; and the summer brought a glut of tomatoes – I can still remember my mother and her friend packing hundreds of them into cardboard boxes to bottle, or to boil up in endless quantities of pasta sauce because we wouldn't see a tomato again before the next summer – and courgettes, which the neighbours thought were frightfully exotic in 1970s Ireland, almost as if my mother were growing cannabis plants instead of small marrows; and then there were endless successions of what my father used to gleefully refer to as 'eejits' – there was Gooseberry eejit, raspberry eejit, strawberry eejit, lovely fruity, creamy summer desserts that came from the back garden, not from Peru via Tesco Finest.

But much as I eulogize my childhood food memories,

it's tempting to forget just how cheerfully my mother embraced processed food, having spent far too long stewing beef and boiling bacon during the 1970s. 'Progress' for her would mean liberation from cross-hatch icing with a piping bag, from the three-course dinner to be prepared every night. As I grew up, I became an avid fan of the oven chip, instant steamed pudding and Bird's Trifle. Anything dehydrated was wildly popular in our family and was my absolute favourite because if I ate it I could pretend that I was on my very own lunar mission. Manna from heaven was provided by instant mashed potato, fake cream and freeze-dried curry, or everyone's favourite, Angel Delight, a custard-like confection which contained not one 'real' ingredient, being made up instead of 'E' numbers – with which we saw nothing wrong. 'E' numbers to us meant liberation from corned beef and overcooked vegetables.

And now, thirty years later, we are learning to embrace 'real food' again, to ditch the conveniences that our mothers so cheerfully embraced and to make home-cooked nourishing food, based on real ingredients, not the panic-bought instant stuff to be eaten in the rush after work and school. The bacon, cabbage and potatoes, stews and mince of my childhood have now been replaced by five-a-day, wholegrains and fish oils; the mark of our decency as parents is whether we prepare our children's dinners from scratch, or, horrors, reach into the freezer for another batch of fish fingers.

In spite of all we know about food and nutrition now, with time the new commodity that defines our lives as mothers, we have less opportunity than ever to nourish our children. My mother and grandmother had time to cook because their lives were to a certain extent separate from their children's. They weren't circling suburban neighbourhoods in their cars like planes coming into Heathrow, dropping Jane and Peter off to karate, swimming, tennis, piano, or standing over their children as they did their homework. I flick through recipe books, wishing that I had the time to bake the delicious-sounding orange mini cakes on p. 253, if I could squeeze in a moment between trying to edit a script, supervise homework, stick something on for dinner that isn't instant, take a phone call from a client, etc., drop someone to a party or to scouts, etc. From filling every moment, food and domestic life is now packed into the crevices of a busy day.

*

When I was a child, my mother passed, or attempted to pass, her knowledge on to me, because that's what you did, to ensure that your daughter would be equipped with the necessary skills to maintain her own home and to be a fine, upstanding housewife in her own right. My mother taught me to fold sheets, both of us folding and folding again, holding on to the outside corners of the sheet, until we were left with a long rectangle, which we would fold in half by marching towards each other, holding the sheet up to meet the other half. I now fold sheets by bundling them up into a ball and hurling them to the top of the airing cupboard as I am too small to reach the top shelf. She taught me to thread and sew with her Singer sewing machine, which was operated by a pressure pad on a flex beside the machine, rather like a mouse. I used to delight in pressing the button too fast and watching the material race through under the needle, until the thread caught up into a huge tangle and my mother politely suggested I stop.

She also taught me how to bake cakes, how to measure out the ingredients into the goblet-shaped shiny measuring cup that she'd brought home from a trip to America in the 1950s. Before we started, she would carefully peruse Maura Laverty's *Full and Plenty*, so used by my mother that the edges of this simple hardback cookbook were frayed, and when she opened them to consult a recipe, bits of paper fell out, with scribbled recipes for scones and bread and chicken casseroles on them. Laverty's recipes were long on narrative, with a little story from her own life, charmingly illustrating a scone recipe or that for a beef stew; the book contained nothing other than a few black-and-white photos of scones and jam sponge and yet it was a classic of Irish home-baked food and culture. Once we'd selected the recipe, my mother would pass on tips about folding flour into the egg, butter and sugar mixture with a spatula so as not to beat the air out, and when adding egg to the creamed butter and sugar to sprinkle in a pinch of flour as well to stop the eggs curdling. There are so many things I think that I instinctively do in my own cooking that I realize my mother must have taught me. Without knowing it, I unconsciously soaked up her domestic skills, so that they became the blueprint for my own, rather less perfect ones.

What I miss most of all as a mother, with all of my children, is the sharing of time that these quiet tasks demand. How to fit in a cookery lesson amongst the improving piano lessons to which I must drop them, the extra karate on a Friday, the endless carefully arranged playdates because going out on the road to play is no longer an option? How to be patient in the mixing and the chopping when we have to rush to get out to scouts, or dinner has to be swiftly prepared after swimming and before choir practice? And how do I connect with my daughter with no batches of scones to make or bacon to boil? In our twenty-first-century way, my daughter and I treat ourselves to a browse around the shops, where she plants ideas in my mind about things she really wants and I silently decide which ones I will give in to and which ones carefully ignore. Or we might go for coffee and cake together and I delight in seeing her pick the Oreo Cookie hot chocolate, the one that comes with melting Oreo cookies – as it should be, I feel. But when I read Con Houlihan's charming description of a little girl's breadmaking in the *ICA Cookbook*, I regret that shopping and doing 'stuff' has come to replace the quieter bonding moments.[12]

I feel connected to my mother's and grandmother's experience of motherhood in a unique way, as so many of my memories are filled with the minutiae of domestic routine, the things we did together, the silly questions that could be asked whilst making a batch of scones, the chats that could be had about all manner of subjects, quietly thinking that my mother knew just about everything, marvelling at the peculiar concoctions of methylated spirits and vinegar that Nana would apply to just about any household surface. In the frenzy of activity that packs our days, it can be hard to fit in time to do quiet things with my children that don't involve consumption and frenzied activity, or spending large amounts of money on events, to bake a batch of banana muffins that fail to rise above the edge of the muffin case, or some rubbery jam tarts or to cremate some flapjacks, whilst my children fight over who is going to lick the wooden spoon.

*

What I mourn rather less is the opportunity to pass on essential womanly skills to my daughter, in the expecta-

12. 'In the old days, every little girl began her career as a baker by making a Cisteen Baise. She begged her mother to give her some of the dough she was kneading and then shaped it in her hands and put it in the oven with the parent cake.' Con Houlihan commentaries in the *ICA Cookbook* (ICA, 1960).

tion that she will be doing exactly the same thing twenty years from now. I do the occasional bit of mending and have carefully demonstrated to all my children how the thread goes in the needle, but it has been my daughter who has expressed an interest in what I'm doing, rather than my son, who has pronounced it all 'yucky'. And whilst my son wrestled unhappily with the knitting of a St Patrick's Day scarf aged eight, my daughter cheerfully repeats the knitting rhyme 'In through the bunny hole, around the oak tree, out through the bunny hole and off goes he', whilst attempting to knit a scarf for Teddy. To my daughter, it is important that Mummy teach her stuff; whether it be card games or crochet, it's part of our bonding as mother and daughter. But the essential difference is that, to me and my daughter, these skills are no longer necessary to forge ahead in life, no longer prized as evidence that we are achievers, if only on the domestic front. A pattern has been broken, of passing domestic skills on from mother to daughter: perhaps the shackles of domestic oppression have, at last, been broken?

I'm not so sure. As a young, liberated woman, living in Paris after college, smoking a lot of cigarettes and teaching English to earn a crust, filling my diaries with visits to cafés and museums, eking out a *café-crème* because I'd paid the exorbitant price of twenty francs for it, I never thought that my life would come to mirror my mother's so closely. We were the post-feminist generation, no longer slaves to the oven and the washing line like our own mothers. And yet, here I am, in the world of drudge, the daily emptying of the laundry basket, the filling of the dishwasher, the making of vast amounts of food, the daily routine not greatly changed since 1947. Did I go to college and negotiate the finer points of Hegel's dialectic to spend my time unearthing the stash of dirty underpants and socks that my son has stuffed down the side of his bed rather than into the laundry basket? Are we the generation of mothers who left Stepford behind only to find ourselves quietly imprisoned by it again? And how the hell did that happen?

Well, there's the simple fact that more women stay at home with their children than men, and thus more women end up doing the daily chores, the hoovering, washing and shopping, leaving the weekend chores – the masculine chopping of wood, fixing of shelving and trips to the recycling centre – to their partners; and even when both work, women still do most of the housework, it's a fact,[13] whilst men are still extravagantly praised if they lift the Hoover – 'Tim's so *good*, isn't he, to help out?' – or worse, are forbidden from doing housework by their spouses in case they do too much damage, as one commentator to a talkboard noted: 'He has ruined too many loads of laundry mixing colors, broken too many dishes "helping out" after dinner, doesn't know how to

---

13. Source: *Journal of Family Issues*, 2002, in *USA Today*; the *Daily Telegraph*, the *Daily Mail*.

stack a dish washer to save his life, can't find anything, doesn't know how to turn on the vacuum cleaner and his idea of cleaning something is scary.'

And the great irony of all the labour-saving devices that would take us out of the kitchen is that they have resulted in higher standards at precisely the time when we have less time to achieve them and less help than ever before. Unlike middle-class women in Nana's time, who would have had a live-in housekeeper to fill the range with turf and polish the silver, Nana didn't have one, because she was terrified that she might bring TB into the house with her, as it was rampant in Ireland at the time and Nana's beloved sister Carmel had died from it. She did, however, avail herself of a 'daily', a young girl from the town who hadn't been lured away to the pottery, the town's main employer. My father lived alone with his grandfather and, as two men were deemed incapable of looking after themselves, they had housekeepers of varying quality. But gradually, the acceptability of hiring help changed and whilst many of my mother's contemporaries had silent Spanish girls to help out while they went off to play golf, or do the shopping, my mother saw getting a cleaning lady or a housekeeper as a sign that you were a bit lazy – sure what else would you have to do all day? Now, we agonize over whether to hire that nice Latvian girl and spend our time giving her bonuses and plane tickets back to Riga because we feel so guilty about exploiting the poor. And I know plenty of women who clean their houses diligently before the cleaner turns up, in order to avoid embarrassment. Far from being liberated from household tasks in the cheerful, politically incorrect manner of our parents, we are bound to do even more of them.

*

But is my identity still bound up with how shiny the kitchen tiles are and how many washes I've put on this week? Well, yes, in a way. Just like my mother and grandmother, this is my 'job' – the home, the kids, and I want to make sure that my children are fed, clothed and bathed with reasonable frequency, and that the place doesn't look like a complete tip.

For Mum and Nana, the domestic sphere was one where they could achieve excellence. As a member of the Irish Countrywomens Association, whose remit was to keep alive the traditional homemaking skills of country life, Nana excelled at domestic activities with a rural twist: the curing of leather to make into one of her Fresian handbags; the making of tablemats out of rush-work, an intricate pattern of interwoven brown strands, carefully varnished, sitting under our breakfast cereal bowls; there was the fire-stand in the shape of a Tara brooch, which would be carefully placed in front of the fireplace when the fire was out. Many of the skills Nana possessed would be considered hilariously unnecessary nowadays – badger-skin foot rest, anyone? – but Nana was a kind of Irish Inuit, at one with nature and using it to feed and clothe herself in an immediate way. My mother used her many homemaking skills, her knitting, gardening, sewing, baking, to demonstrate her mastery of the domestic life she enjoyed at a time when little else was open to her. She seems to have knitted her way through my childhood, recalling a fishing trip with Dad where they hired a boat and took it out on a windswept lake for the day: while Dad cast off and tied flies onto the end of the fishing line, my mother sat at the other end of the boat knitting a matinee coat for my brother.

I consider housework and food preparation a necessary evil, a part of life which is 'there' in the same way as tax returns and the common cold. I mop, clean, wash, hoover, only because not to would result in my house looking like a student bedsit, and because I take a certain amount of grim pride in conquering the smelly microwave or the rotting vegetation at the bottom of the fridge – a sign that I am in control of the domestic sphere. But mine is absolutely a no-frills service, the Ryanair approach to housework: I don't undertake any major spring-clean kind of activity, as this would involve wasting time when I could be otherwise engaged in a nice book or watching a movie, or going to the park; I have trained my children to accept odd socks as to match them requires effort I am unwilling to expend. I haven't ironed in five years, unless for a special occasion, and the kitchen drawers are full of a jumble of bits of old string, odd domestic implements, combs, hair bands, school reports, etc. – if it is hidden, it doesn't exist, as far as I am concerned. For me, domestic life is something I must execute to a minimum standard to avoid embarrassment – I may not live in a show home, but it is reasonably clean – and I take no pleasure in it whatsoever.

The pride that my mother and grandmother took in home-based activities is clearly not part of my genetic inheritance and I have to admit to feeling a certain amount of embarrassment at this, that I am such a 'failure', but is this simply because I feel I should, as a woman, possess these skills innately? After all, it's just work at the end of the day, isn't it? Someone's got to do it – for six years it was my husband, and now it's me. Instead of kicking the photocopier, I'm kicking the vacuum cleaner; instead of poring over another bloody spreadsheet, I'm trying to work out when my eldest doesn't have swimming.

An older woman friend, on hearing about my decision to leave office work, said to me, 'Well, it's great that you can use those management skills you learned in the office at home with the children,' and my hair stood on end. What on earth did she mean? Did she seriously think that running around after three children could even compare to the cut and thrust of office life? It was enough to rile my every feminist instinct, that I'd gone to college to manage the playdate schedules of my children. But she's right in a way – I have to use similar skills to talk my five-year-old out of scoffing a whole packet of jellies as I would talking an author out of a strop over a dodgy set of proofs. It's all a slog, really.

But the thing is, one slog is definitely valued more than another. Keeping the home together, the children fed and clothed, has been devalued because it's something women generally do and therefore not important; in the same way as liking clothes and shoes is 'trivial' and watching Premiership matches isn't. At least in my mother's time, the deification of the housewife meant that she could feel good about her clean cooker top, her perfectly baked apple pie, ignoring the fact that she was part of a global conspiracy to keep her knitting away in the corner, not storming into the male territory of the boardroom. Which is why I find the current creeping Martha Stewart-ization of domestic life so interesting. All those lovely American ladies extolling the virtues of French polishing and cleaning parquet flooring with a toothbrush, the filling of hand-woven baskets with home-grown flowers or hand-baked cookies, the reclaiming of the comforting value of knitting, the quiet rituals of which so tortured me as a child, with my wonky tea-cosies and slipped stitches. Are these women reclaiming traditional skills and celebrating them, or slyly implying that women who possess these skills are somehow superior, better mothers, better at 'pleasing' their husbands, not rocking the boat with nasty old liberation and all of the muddle which ensues?

*

In two generations, my family's experience of mother-hood has moved from urban to rural to urban again, and from the privations of the Second World War to the shiny consumption of the blessed Celtic Tiger. And although the quality of domestic endeavour has changed hugely during that time, the core of domestic life, the daily grind of meal production and house cleaning, has changed rather less. But that's life: the small daily rituals of washing, cleaning and cooking will always be with us, along with gas bills, tax returns and car insurance. Children generate mess that needs to be cleaned up, they demand food and clothing, not unreasonably, and someone's got to provide it. But the dismal fact that it is still so much a woman's responsibility is rather less cheering.

Over the past five years, I have come to terms with my domestic responsibilities. I grimly execute them simply because I am here and it is thus simpler for me to drag the vacuum cleaner out of the cupboard under the stairs than to ring my husband and demand that he returns home from the office to do so; the same goes for dinner-making which falls naturally, if unhappily, into my afternoon routine. Whether this is an assault on my feminist principles is something I have to accept, as I thrust the shopping list into my husband's hands so that he can visit the supermarket on a Monday night after dropping the kids off at scouts. But the assumption that I will enjoy this daily grind, and want to turn it into a shrine to my achievements as a woman, it being the only thing I can do, is rather less present in my life. I don't feel demeaned as a woman because I have to put a wash on, but instead feel that I'm doing what needs to be done to keep the show on the road: perhaps I should feel inferior, but I don't, as I have plenty of other things to be getting on with, thanks to the efforts of my mother's and grandmother's generations. The question *Who am I?* that I asked myself five years ago has been answered to my own reasonable satisfaction and, no, the answer isn't 'housewife' or 'worker bee' but mother, editor, writer, daughter, partner. And as my baby turns five and heads out the door to primary school for the first time, or my son begins secondary school, that question will change again and again after that as life happens and things change around me and memories of the constantly humming washing machine and socks drying on the radiator fade.

Take It from Me

* We all have our own ways of negotiating the drudgery of domestic life, whether it be hiring a cleaning lady or insisting on doing it all ourselves, and whatever gets it done is just fine. And it doesn't matter how you divide the chores, as long as they get done.

* We all need to let ourselves off the hook about some convenience for our time-pressured lives as mothers.

A lot of people have reacted strongly to Delia Smith's *How to Cheat at Cooking*, with her plastic onions and, horrors, tinned mince, but behind the opprobrium lie the unrealistic high standards of the Freshists, with the idea being constantly rammed down our throats that only green, organic produce, ideally hand-picked by Papua New Guinean tribesmen, will suffice for our families. To serve them anything else is sacrilege and if you dare insert a fish finger into Ollie's orifice, you are probably as good as poisoning him; but Delia may have a point: family food should be convenient as well as nutritious.

* Try to ignore your mother's or mother-in-law's comments about the state of the place, her 'innocent' questions about whether you've ever thought of doing a bit of dusting and when was the last time you cleaned the fridge; smile sweetly and tell her you'll be getting around to it soon, you're sure. We know that times have changed and we can no longer throw our children out in the rain so that we can polish the silver, but try to bite back the urge to inform her that unlike her, you have better things to be doing with your time than folding socks – save that rant for your partner when you can let rip about what an old bat she is.

* Housework is a chore, and no one would argue otherwise, even if dusting and cleaning gives us

satisfaction; but other domestic tasks like cooking and baking can be good opportunities for quiet time with our children, for getting essential information out of them about what's going on in school or what their friends are up to and how horrible the new maths teacher is. As a mother I am frequently only half-listening to their chat as I busy myself with the endless chores of the day, so such oases of talk and 'active' listening are welcome.

* Nowadays, domestic tasks are no longer uniquely Mother's duty, showing that she is in control of her lovely home, nor is slavery to children's mess and detritus. I struggle every day to get my children to help out, to lay the table and fill the dishwasher, to make their beds – hauling one whole duvet up over their pillows – and to tidy up under their beds. But I keep on at it, reminding myself of all the unpleasant slobs with whom I shared flats as a young woman, whose mothers had clearly not trained them in the same diligent manner, and what a nightmare they were. Sharing domestic chores is about more than just lessening the drudgery, but about learning to have some consideration for others, essential life skills.

Chapter Seven

What Kind of Mother Am I?

'If only motherhood ended with the cutting of the umbilical cord, we'd be cruising.'

Susan Maushart, *The Mask of Motherhood*, (Penguin, 1999)

'The true mother has no thought of self. All her life, all her love, are given to her husband and children and after them and because of them, to all and everything that have need of her.'

Nora Tynon O'Mahony, 'The Mother', in *Maria Luddy, Women in Ireland 1800–1918*

Last year, a letter on headed notepaper arrived home from school. Underneath the bright cheery logo of a child holding some balloons, the letter announced that our then-nine-year-old son had been selected for a nationwide survey on being a child in Ireland today.

Enthusiastically, we agreed to participate in the survey, not exactly realizing the extent of the gruelling question-naire to which we would be subjected for a whole two hours one Monday night while the dinner burned quietly on the stove. A little man called Michael came through the door, pulling behind him a wheelie suitcase containing a thick book of questions to ask my son and myself, a sheaf of brightly coloured forms on which to record son's daily activities and a weighing scales which I looked at in horror – this definitely wasn't part of the plan. Nonethe-less, I cheerfully answered the detailed questions, silently congratulating myself on what a great mother I was, how solicitous of my child's welfare, how interested in his development. I answered questions about whether he had more than one pair of shoes (no, actually, as he refuses to wear trainers and I'm too stingy to buy him anything else), and whether he ate one hot meal a day and whether I'd ever struggled to pay the leccy bill. I even got on the bloody scales – would I describe myself as being slightly, moderately or considerably overweight, Michael asked me. I shot him a murderous look. And then it was my son's turn, and we tried not to eavesdrop as Michael asked him searching questions about play and family life, my son murmuring slightly mystified responses as his mother hadn't actually filled him in on what he might be asked to do beforehand. Dutifully, he filled out a mysterious pink sheet, solemnly etching out the words in pencil.

Later that evening, my son revealed that, during his questioning, on a scale of one to ten, he had rated me about a five, and told Michael that he got on 'fairly well' with me. Not brilliantly, not even very well, but *fairly* well. I felt my stomach sink. How could my picture of myself as a mother have been so radically different to my son's? Why, to my son, was I not Mother of the Year, after all I'd bloody done for him?

It was a chastening experience. After all, I had 'sacrificed' my career to spend valuable time with my children, so that they could benefit from my presence at home and flourish under my careful tutelage, and they simply weren't grateful enough. Or was it me? Was I basically a crap mother? A period of soul-searching ensued, all the bad decisions I'd made coming back to me in uncomfortable detail. I began to ask myself how my children must see me, how their memories are being shaped as they grow and what they will remember when they get older – the golden years of a happy childhood or something rather less lovely? And, deep down, I wondered, with a jolt of discomfort, if I had maintained the tradition of strong, eccentric women in my family, almost too much for their children, like undiluted maternal whiskey. I wondered how much of my mothering comes down to the way my mother mothered me, hidden under layers of dutiful twenty-first-century political correctness, but there nonetheless, making itself felt as I grow older and slowly become my mother.

*

Who am I as a mother? I've tried to be honest here. I know that I'm affectionate, loving my children's hugs and kisses and hugging and kissing them back. I'm interested in my children, in how they see the world, what they like and loathe, what their talents are: to me, my children are the brightest and most gorgeous in the world, which is entirely as it should be. I am reasonably entertaining at times, happy to join in ABBA disco sessions and to hold a skipping rope. I will even kick a football around in a totally cack-handed manner. I like baking things with them – mainly because I like eating the results – and I don't get too worked up about mess. I'm not terribly pushy: at their karate class, I watch their moves with interest and don't get overly excited if they aren't Grand

Master Ding-dong after a few months. Am I not great? What an exemplary and rounded mother I am.

Lie. I am also horribly impatient and can often be found banging the desk as my son flails around with his maths homework – not because of the work, but because of his inability to do it in less than two hours, or when he whines that he can't find his swimming gear again, or that my daughter takes a half an hour to brush her hair and select a pair of matching socks every school morning. I am a drama queen, choosing to get upset and storm off at their behaviour, or throw myself into a temper, shrieking at them like a fishwife, rather than deal with it – after all, I am the adult in the house; and I'm terminally inconsistent, announcing draconian rules to curb wayward behaviour and then forgetting all about them. My children's pocket money isn't a carefully organized reward for carrying out chores, but instead an occasional dive into the purse and a flinging of disparate sums of money at them for chores that are often carried out by a mother who simply can't face another battle over tidying up Lego and figures it's easier to do it herself.

And sometimes, to my shame, I haven't been the ally they needed, the mother they deserve. At times, this has been brought home to me in painful ways. I have made many mistakes as a parent, some minor, some terribly crass, but as mothering happens so much in the moment, we tend to bury it all and simply move along to the next day. But a general pattern emerges: many of my mistakes come from misunderstanding my children and who they are, from putting expediency ahead of their needs, from finding myself unconsciously repeating the mistakes of the past or from pursuing an idealized version of motherhood and punishing myself and my children when the reality turns out to be entirely different.

My eldest son loves reading, science and computers and even though his lively sense of humour guarantees that he has plenty of friends who find his rugby allergy entertaining, by his own cheerful admission he isn't even remotely group-oriented or sporty, and yet he regularly undergoes the purgatory of the cub scout weekend, a festival of organized activity and manic good cheer which he loathes. And yet, I insist he attend this outpouring of jollity and he rings me every five minutes on his mobile to tell me how little he's enjoying himself. I find myself biting back the impatience, willing him to just get on with it, although privately I can understand why he doesn't, being similarly allergic to organized 'fun' activity: the horrors of kayaking, drifting across a chilly expanse of water, hoping I won't capsize/lose an oar/drift into the bushes and make a complete eejit of myself; the manic good cheer of the campfire sing-song when really I'd like to curl up with a good book, the constant damp backside from slithering down rocks and, worst of all, the bloody team-building. Why on earth would I want to build a raft with other people to demonstrate that I am a rounded person, capable of getting on with others – we can just as easily sit down and have a nice cup of tea and a peruse of *Hello!*. The thing is, if I understand the horrors of the whole thing, why don't I let him dodge the awfulness? Because scout camps are 'good for him', they will form his little character, providing him with self-confidence and outdoor skills should he ever need to survive in the wilderness beyond Dublin 6: such activities are what children do, after all, part of the idealized version of childhood we all hold in our heads: 'Five Go Down to the Woods'.

And then there is trying not to be critical of my daughter in the way only mothers can be – the remarks about dress and appearance which are never made to our sons and which guarantee that the chafing, too-close relationship, full of irritation and suppressed rage, is passed on from mother to daughter. Like many eight-year-old girls, my daughter dresses in an interesting mix of things that don't go together and items that she wore when she was five but can't bear to part with, even though they are now several sizes too small for her: one pair of sequinned pink wedge-heeled sandals that she wore to a wedding three years ago are now so small she can't even squeeze her feet into them. So she has cut off the strap that went around the ankle and now wears them as a pair of mules. Lovely. And I congratulate myself that, at long last, I have learned to say nothing, except that they look wonderful and isn't she terribly clever to have thought of extending their wear like that, trying not to listen as she clack-clacks up and down the hall like a pageant queen.

My new-found *sagesse* comes after a series of battles about what I consider to be inappropriate dress, mortified by her choice of leggings-with-holes-in-them and three-year-old-T-shirt combo for friends' birthday parties. Why couldn't she wear something respectable? I would often challenge, and if she didn't cooperate, a temper tantrum would ensue – mine, that is. It took me a while, and a few tears on her part, to work out that the issue here was not her decision to wear a pair of leggings and a T-shirt – after all, so what? – but my embarrassment that my daughter would attend a posh party dressed like a mini Max Wall. Faced with the spectre of my own snobbery and also with the prospect of turning into the kind of mother who criticized her daughter constantly – a novel concept, I know – I have generally learned to bite my tongue. When she was getting her ears pierced, I applauded her choice of earrings, the biggest blingest fake-diamond earrings in the shop, and told her they were gorgeous, and they were on her tiny little face, their David Beckhamesque size being no obstacle to her loveli-ness. This was her moment and I'd just have to suck it up.

And then there's my relationship with my youngest, fiery and affectionate in equal measure, a battle of the wills with shouts and screams being followed by hugs and kisses, dire threats being followed by profuse apologies and promises to do better from both parties. Since the day he was born, our relationship has been loving, but full of fireworks. His childhood has been affected more by the tensions in my mothering that come from balancing work and family life. Over the years, no matter whether I've worked from home or office, I have felt the teeth-gnashing guilt of putting work before child, or the disapproving scrutiny of some when I place my children before a sales meeting or an evening book launch. I still shudder at the thought that I persisted in sending my zippy little firebrand to a rigid nursery school which he royally hated because the hours and the location suited me better than the sweet little pre-school that he had been attending but which was far away from his siblings' primary school and only open until twelve. And for my sins I had to endure – as did he – a constant litany of complaints about his behaviour, which grew by the day: how he didn't colour within the lines – *really*, could that be because he is not yet even three? How he helped himself to juice and raisins because he didn't know any better, or lunged at the crayons at colouring time instead of placing his hands on his knees and asking nicely. And even though I really wanted to tell them to shove it up their anally-retentive, wooden-toy-using asses, for the sake of a particularly difficult work project I persisted in sending him to his own personal hell-hole. 'He's a bit aggressive, I know,' I murmured, begging the teacher to take him back for another couple of weeks. I did move him to a lovely new pre-school, after both he and I had been left in tears following a particularly lacerating encounter, but the guilt stays with me. 'I hated my old school, Mum,' he cheerfully reminds me from time to time. I know, I think, and it's all my fault.

*

I always use my son's experience to beat myself up when I think about being a working mother, whether from home or office – that and the purgatory of those summer-holiday mornings when I have to get a piece on key autumn trends in the book industry into the books page to which I contribute, bellowing at my beloveds to keep the noise down and nodding my head distractedly at the constant requests for chocolate biscuits because it'll keep them quiet for a few minutes. The irony isn't lost on me that I have replaced the firm routines of the office for a rather-less-ideal shuttle between study, i.e. bedroom, and kitchen, neither with my children nor separate from them – the worst of both worlds. So much for staying at home the better to devote myself to them.

And yet, the notion of stay-at-home mothering as the zenith of maternal achievement is a relatively recent phenomenon. Many mothers used to work, handing their children over to Granny and heading off to the factory or the shop-floor, or the café counter. Working mothers were an accepted part of the mothering reality. Irish country mothers were always working, feeding livestock and helping to herd and milk cattle and running the household, as much a partner in the family business as their husbands. And then in my grandmother's time, with lots more money around, relatively speaking, the role of the stay-at-home mother came into its own, the domestic goddess feeding and caring for her family, keeping the house spotless and providing love and care to her children, as well as an endless supply of fun activities. For my mother, stay-at-home motherhood was an inevitability, something to be aspired to, a sign of status that she didn't 'have to work'; that Dad was able to provide for her so that she could do her motherly duty and stay at home: talking to her, it is clear that she never envisaged any other future.

But her stay-at-home and mine are not the same. When Mum was a young mother, she was there in the background, doing something whilst we got on with the business of being children. Making dinner on top of the stove while Ian and I played our favourite game of television at her feet, with the newsreader framed by the clear-glass door of the cooker and the 'audience' pretending to pay attention. She would knit silently in the corner while Ian and I raced cars over the living-room carpet; or doze with her feet up in front of the fire on wet Sunday afternoons, refusing to wake up even when we started jumping on the furniture. To Mum, being a stay-at-home mother meant exactly that, staying at home; it didn't mean standing over her children applauding their every minor achievement, or enthusiastically joining in their games.

The glorification of the role of stay-at-home mother persists now, in the twenty-first century, but with a new and demanding twist. It has become the gold standard by which 'good motherhood' is measured. The really 'good' mothers are those who wait patiently at home for their children, home-baked goodies in hand, sports kit neatly pressed, always ready to wipe a dirty nose or listen to an anecdote. They are always free to do the party run, or to fill the swimming lesson rota; they are fully up to speed with what's going on at school, unlike the harried working mums who just put in the odd appearance at the school concert. They know all about the correct nutrition for their children's optimum development, they take them willingly to piano lessons and wait whilst their little one perfects Rachmaninov's Piano Concerto No. 2. because they are *so* advanced. The implication is clear: those who stay at home with their children are better mothers, putting their children's needs before their own; those who work are not — after all, how can your children possibly come first if you are out at the office all day and not waiting patiently to service your children's needs?

Perhaps Mum and Nana were right to leave us to our own devices, to work things out for ourselves, to roam the streets of our suburban childhoods encountering danger and testing right from wrong by simple trial and error. But of course, it's not really about whether we work or stay at home, but about how we balance our children's needs against our own, and this has nothing to do with our readiness with the ham-and-cheese sandwiches and nourishing smoothies. How do I balance my own need for privacy, for a bit of peace and quiet, with theirs to explore their environment, i.e. make a mess and constantly ask me what I'm doing now? How do I foster my children's independence when I am at home and therefore able to supply them with a packed lunch, a hot breakfast, their uniform produced for them every morning, their beds made? Children can assume that you are doing all of this simply because you have nothing else to do. Where does nurturing stop and spoiling begin?

And working mothers are never going to snap at their youngest to 'leave me alone for five minutes, for God's sake', because they have been pestered for hours upon end with a roster of trivial complaints, grumbles, moans, etc.; they are delighted to have their time at home in the evenings and will cheerfully bathe infants without bellowing at them not to splash water all over the bathroom floor; they are never going to completely lose it at seven-thirty every evening – as do I – because they literally cannot bear to be in the presence of their little darlings for another second, having endured quite enough of them all day. Their needs for intellectual fulfillment and social interaction have been met and as a result they are smiling and patient at the end of the day, not secretly wondering if they could just walk out the door for a bit and come back and find that the last ten years have been erased and that they are now single, wealthy and themselves once more, to spend an evening in front of the telly, glass of wine in hand . . .

I thought that staying at home with my children would make me a better mother, but it hasn't. I'm simply a different mother. And whether I am at home knitting quietly or at work seventy hours a week, I am the mother I am. I really do try my best.

And listing all of the ways in which I am a deficient mother achieves nothing, I realize. All the accumulated 'Careful, you'll drop that's and 'How many times have I told you's, all the 'Here, you're doing it all wrong's, an inventory of failure and inadequacy on which it is futile to dwell. I recognize within myself a dramatic, quick personality, a quixotic impatience, an overbearing quality at times, an ability to bustle into a peaceful room and upset the quiet equilibrium by demanding sock-folding and doing of homework and asking my children searching questions that they have no desire to answer. That I can be a bit of a dragon sometimes isn't new, and I can also be loving and enthusiastic – the same mixture of qualities and defects as any other mother. After all, no mother is perfect.

*

But what has become uncomfortably clear to me the longer I mother is the extent to which I have become my mother, and, yes, Nana, in my own mothering. Turning into our mothers is our great fear as mothers, the spectre that looms in the shadows of our own mothering, haunting our every barked command or sarcastic comment, our every old wives' utterance. And at a more fundamental level, our experience of being mothered shapes our views on educating our children, disciplining them, their religion, politics and even our mothering itself. Turning into our mothers seems to be an inevitable part of the mothering process as we unconsciously mimic our closest female role model, but it is something against which we chafe: our genetic inheritance is something we both loathe and dread.

Even a full nine years after her death, it's hard for my mother to talk about her mother without becoming faintly hysterical. As she reminisces, her voice grows gradually more and more shrill. The picture that emerges of her mother, of a zany, irrepressible show-off with a penchant for dressing up, talking endlessly no matter if you were listening to her or not, of the bewildering inappropriateness of much of what she said, the determination to be the centre of attention which was often so wearying, the way she constantly slightly misunderstood the world and would therefore get it all slightly wrong, is entirely accurate. When my mother talks about her mother, mortification is never far away.

It's true that many of my memories of Nana are accompanied by the hot flush of embarrassment: at the gigantic headdress she prepared for my first Holy Communion as she thought it would give me – aged seven – a 'bit of height'; or the time she presented my sister, aged thirteen, with a series of see-through chiffon nighties to accompany her on her exchange trip to France. The logic seemed to be that the French might appreciate them, they being such a sophisticated lot. Present-giving would be accompanied by the list of things she had 'nearly' bought us, all of which sounded infinitely more appealing than the stuffed stoat I received on one occasion, mounted on a rather handsome moss-covered base. 'I knew that you liked animals,' she trilled. Yes, I thought, when they're *alive*. For birthdays, Christmases, etc., we would either receive a large wad of money or a rather mangy second-hand jacket in the wrong size, depending on her mood. My sister suffered particularly, as Nana seemed to have appointed her as her fashion inheritor and inflicted on her a variety of handmedowns, many of which came complete with their previous owner's whiff. However, I also remember great kindness, a warm sense of humour and a delight in laughing at herself, as well as the aforementioned quixotic generosity, which was highly amusing or offensive, depending on your point of view.

The thing is, she wasn't *my* mother.

As her beloved only daughter and therefore the focus of Nana's entire being, my mother was also made to wear inappropriate headgear, in this case huge white bows in her hair, when all her friends had sensible hairbands, and frilly, fussy dresses when all others wore plain woollen pinafores; when Mum and her friends would dress up to go trick or treating at Hallowe'en, Nana would come too, dressed up in some outlandish costume which was guaranteed to embarrass her only child, as were her obvious attempts to hog the limelight. When my mother had a row with her friends, she never had the opportunity to sort it out before Nana would leap in and intervene. And, as my mother was her only child, Nana poured every ounce of her energies into her development – this bright-eyed scrutiny, the unrealistic expectations of talent and genius would have been too much for any child to bear, and certainly too much for my mother. 'I had to be the girl to my mother and the boy to my father,' she added. 'I always felt the responsibility of that.'

To a certain extent my mother has created herself in opposition to Nana: where Nana was flamboyant, my mother is restrained; where Nana liked fashion, my mother has opted for sensible trousers and jumpers and good walking shoes. Unlike Nana, she was not moved to wear sequinned boob tubes when they came into fashion (albeit worn with a tasteful chiffon jacket, a nod to her age. My sister, of course, inherited the ancestral boob tube when Nana had finished with it). And Nana's wilful adoration of trash culture, with her only concession to reading being Mills & Boon, contrasted strongly with my mother's love of classical music and Jane Austen, and yet, as mothers, they shared more than they might have liked to admit.

The gene for eccentricity was certainly passed down from mother to daughter, as my mother had a series of fixed views about the world which she didn't keep to herself and which would cause us quietly to roll our eyes to heaven as children. *Top of the Pops* could never be watched in peace in our household without Mum going on about how German experimental group Kraftwerk all looked like Fascists and should be ashamed of themselves, or how African-American soul singers 'all sound the same, you know'. Then there was the annual St Patrick's Day mortification of being dispatched to pick the front lawn of our local shop in search of shamrocks, in full view of the neighbours, not to mention the bemused shop assistant, because my mother didn't see why we should pay for them like normal people. But such are the eccentricities of any mother – my husband, for example, cheerfully tells me that he and his siblings were made to wear Wellington boots at all times between the ages of five and ten – and indeed I share in them, banging on about my pet subjects at any opportunity and dispatching my children to pick dandelions by the side of the road as they are free food for our rabbits. *Plus ça change.*

But unlike Nana, Mum would no more have dreamed of intervening in our childhood scraps than flying to the moon. She let us get on with our own games and japes without insisting on joining in and, apart from mild admonishments about piano practice, didn't attempt to mould us into anything we might not be, and then be disappointed at the results. I credit my mother with my ability to let my children get on with it and to develop their own interests and abilities, and with a dislike of pushing them to anything to which they are not inclined naturally. And in terms of discipline, where Nana was indulgent, my mother most emphatically was not. We were expected to work hard as children, beavering away at a succession of paper rounds and leaflet drops, which needless to say we resented, but which I now credit with my understanding that hard work yields results. This work ethic I try to instil in my own children, who are similarly unable to sit around for long before mother finds a little job for them. It's clear that my mother's mothering was shaped by her relationship with her own mother; as is mine by my relationship with Mum.

But my mother's mothering was also shaped by different and exceptionally difficult circumstances, which changed her as we grew up and which have also profoundly affected the way in which I mother. As a very young child, I remember my mother's softness, a warm, laughing presence, full of affection: I can still remember her soft coos of alarm when I climbed up to the kitchen cupboards and swigged back a mouthful of vinegar, mistaking it for lemonade, or the time I got hold of a box of matches and decided to try lighting one, or her warm hug when I woke one night and screamed the house down because she had nipped out to the shop for a pint of milk – she sounded so apologetic that I accepted her proffered fig roll with a sniff and settled back down to sleep again.

But over the years, this softness gradually became something else, a distraction, a frazzled weariness at having to expend all of her energies on my brother's needs and the constant vigilance that mothering him demanded, a frustration at life's constant battles. And even though she protests that she didn't have any huge ambitions for herself, I know that she had no real time to develop her own life, to explore her own interests beyond digging the vegetable patch and knitting, as keeping my brother on the straight and narrow absorbed all of her time. 'We weren't a real family,' she said to me wistfully when trying to describe the purgatory of a day out with my brother, constantly looking around in a panic, wondering where on earth he'd got to now: 'The countryside was good,' she smiled, 'because with all of those open fields you could see where he'd got to.'

And then there was spending every day of her life fighting to secure his basic care and education, refusing to be palmed off by the local comprehensive when there was a much more suitable special-needs school to which he could go. And then there were his wearing temper tantrums and the complete obsession with routine, with collecting odd groups of things from cars to Action Men, not resting until every Hornby train carriage had been bought and meticulously labelled. And my mother's responsibility for my brother continued through work and continues now, even when he is forty-five years of age, a grown man, happy in his gardening job, with his own flat, his many interests, his collection of specimen spiders and a substantial – alphabetized – DVD collection.

Of course, my mother's struggles affected her relationship with me. 'You were no trouble,' she will often say to me, and indeed I wasn't, sensing that my mother simply didn't have time to deal with any trouble I might present. Trouble was my brother's job, not mine. I remember his return home in triumph on my father's shoulders one Saturday afternoon, shivering and covered in mud, having fallen into a neighbour's garden pond. I was dispatched to buy a large packet of Kimberley biscuits – a real luxury – and carefully carried them up the stairs to him, along with a cup of lukewarm cocoa. He lay in state in his bed, bright eyes staring at me over the top of the eiderdown, and accepted the proffered gifts with a shrug. I was unsure whether or not he was being punished by being sent to bed, but a large plate of Kimberleys sure looked good to me.

But of course, I never 'acted out' or misbehaved terribly to get my own plate of Kimberleys, literally or metaphorically, because I instinctively knew that it was not an option. Whether I liked it or not, I had to be a good girl. But I adopted my own tactics, a constant low whine which I developed to attract her attention, an eagerness to please, a constant need for praise and reassurance: 'Wasn't I a super girl?' was my mantra as a young child. And later, a crippling gloom and demanding anxiety about exams, the weather, politics, would absorb the attention I felt I had missed. My mother feels the loss of enjoyment of my childhood keenly: 'I couldn't enjoy all of the things you were doing, like your gymnastics and your singing, because I was too busy wondering where Ian would go to school next,' she told me. And I watched my baby sister's cheerful teenage misbehaviour with some envy, wishing that I had been able to do the same instead of holding it all in and then visiting ten years' struggle with depression on my parents.

I say all of this not to unleash my inner adolescent or to extract my Freudian revenge on my poor mother. I don't, can't, feel any sense of grievance for a situation that couldn't be changed, but as I grow older and slowly and inexorably become my mother, I have begun to ask myself how the events and relationships of my childhood have shaped me and the way I mother my own children.

*

As a young mother, I was determined that I would be available to my children in a way that I perceived my mother simply not to be. This judgement of my mother I now realize to be horribly unfair: mothering is a tough job at which she, like me, did her best and her reward was to have her children moan about her, as will be mine, I am sure, when my children are old enough. Nonetheless, the determination, shaped by my own childhood, to offer my children 'something else' has been at the heart of my own mothering, has determined my sometimes unnecessary vigilance, the furious energy that I put into mothering. Of course, I now realize that such a level of dedication and devotion is unrealistic, even inappropriate, but back in the early days, I was in training for an Olympic gold in mothering. I approached it as if it were a project of sorts and my poor unfortunate eldest was my subject. No aspect of my son's development would be left to chance. The house was full to bursting with educational toys, soothing musical compilations and brightly coloured books. At one stage, I got hold of outsize dried beans because I had read that counting and feeling the beans would stimulate my son's intelligence. Indeed, he loved the beans and, not being an orally fixated child, would diligently count them out and find little niches in the house in which to hide them, laying them out carefully with neat spaces in between them, tongue sticking out with concentration, never once succumbing to the urge to eat one of them. But the beans seemed to multiply: behind every crevice, in every plug socket or shoe, or mug, lurked a few beans. I would take a swig of tea and be forced to spit out a large bean and a casual hoover of the house would be constantly interrupted by the tinny whine of the machine as I sucked up another bloody bean. I tried singing and dancing to him myself, like a holiday rep at a Greek resort, a demented CBeebies presenter calling my husband in to look if my eldest so much as farted . . . my poor son was becoming the focus of my entire being, rather like my poor mother became the focus of Nana's.

I was overdoing it because I didn't know how to accept myself as an ordinary mother — it wasn't enough for me to be 'good enough', I had to be extraordinary, just 'perfect', fulfilling my son's every need and ignoring his reluctance to be jollied along. Fortunately for him, he would have two siblings, which prevented me turning completely into Nana, as I physically couldn't provide them all with the Platinum Package of motherhood and they simply had to make do with the supermarket own-brand, with the requisite lack of attention, distracted barked commands and half-finished jigsaws because Mum has had to go off and do something else. And they have been just fine, I know, but I have found it hard to come to terms with the fact that I am less than perfect. Every time I admonish my older two for stuffing their dirty underwear down the side of the bed, or shriek at my youngest with such vigour that he covers his ears against the onslaught I think, Uh-oh, let the bad genie out of the bottle again; the mask of lovely motherhood slips to reveal the monster beneath.

I realize with a jolt that my children are looking to me as a role model and that as well as just banging on about stuff, I need to set a good example. I need to stop ranting at rude people or other drivers who cut me up, dispensing random anger around the city of Dublin; I need to spend in an organized rather than a chaotic manner instead of wittering on about budgeting and then spending every penny I have; I need to share time and ideas with them and provide them with a structure and I need to avoid spoiling them. Like every middle-class child I was sheltered and lived a materially comfortable life, but the access my children have to a tidal wave of 'stuff', the sheer luxury of the entertainment with which they are weekly provided, is breathtaking, and rather than bang on about how it wasn't like that in my day, I try simply to limit it, and to get the idea across that they are lucky and that there is another world out there.

As a difficult and impetuous young woman I would regularly get myself into scrapes and expect my unfortunate parents to bail me out, which they did every single time without a word of complaint, listening to my hysterical phone calls, making soothing noises in spite of their anxiety, and, most importantly, allowing me to get on with making my own mistakes. I hope to do the same for my children. And now, when I am trying to teach them about responsibility and caring, I try not to bang on too much about how I had to care for my brother aged ten. I chafed against the responsibility, having to follow him around all of the time to make sure he didn't get bullied by other kids or having to trek to the building site up the road where he had taken up residence, fascinated by the JCBs and tipper-trucks. I loathed having to look after him and my sister when my mother worked during the summer-holiday mornings, having to break up their fights and make an endless supply of toasted cheese sandwiches. My brother's care demanded constant vigilance on my mother's part and, like many siblings of children with disabilities, I took on more than I wanted sometimes. And so now I find it hard to bite my lip when my older two fight about whose turn it is to feed the rabbits, to avoid the temptation to punish them for the relative ease of their young lives.

And yet, I realize that a large part of my mothering ability comes from the part of myself that learned to care, from an early age. Any qualities of caring or empathy I possess, I credit to an upbringing where I didn't come first and, whilst my inner adolescent might whine about it, I'm thankful for that.

*

Like many mothers with a daughter, my relationship with mine matters in a different way to that with my sons. I know that I will get on, somehow, with my uncomplicated boys, but it is the relationship with my daughter that I feel carries the most risk, that I desperately want to work. Coming from my family stock, with Nana's fraught relationship with her mother, my mother's with Nana, it matters to me more than anything. I know just how much I take after the other women in my family and the dangers implicit in the close, chafing mother–daughter relationship.

Recently, my daughter had a morning off school and we decided to treat ourselves to breakfast in a local café.

She had a white hot chocolate which she found just heavenly and then we bought ourselves a couple of things we didn't need. On the way we chatted about nuns and priests, which topic seemed to be on her mind having seen a member of this endangered species at the local school the day before. 'She was wearing monk's clothes, Mum,' she told me, whereupon we began a conversation about what nuns and priests wear, what the word is for trainee nuns and priests, how long it takes to become a nun or priest, etc. It was one of the nicest couple of hours I've spent in quite a while, and it is all down to her. She is the break with the past: in her calm, serene manner and contented self-possession, she is a remarkably sage character, and differs entirely in temperament from her mother, grandmother and great-grandmother. She does possess our eccentricity, but there the resemblance ends – she is not unpredictable, quixotic or hard to read, she shows off, but only in a normal way, as any happy eight-year-old would; she is clever and competitive, but in a refreshingly un-neurotic way, taking a real pleasure in her achievements. She isn't a strong character either – she is the complete opposite of overbearing and bossy. Where on earth did she come from, I sometimes wonder?

And no, I don't credit myself for this lovely little girl; she is, after all, her own person, but I do thank God that as a mother, I have been able to be open with her, to show her love and affection in a way that was so hard for my mother and grandmother to do when such unseemly displays were frowned upon. And I have been able to relax as a mother with her, knowing that she is valued in school and that her education is taken seriously, that she isn't under the cosh of Sister Benildus, cowed and mute as were we; I assume that a happy future full of possibility lies ahead of my daughter; that she is part of a society that allows women to express themselves, to be something other than stalwart mothers of nine, slaving away to keep their families together. I try to offer my daughter extra love and support because I know something of what lies ahead for her, the challenges that she, and not her brothers, will have to face. I hope that by the time she is grown, the world will have changed enough to allow her to use her education without guilt and to be paid just as much as her male counterparts. I hope that she will achieve everything that she has set out to achieve, whilst I realize that I may be setting her up for disappointment when she learns that everything isn't possible. I hope that she won't need to make the sacrifices that her mother, grandmother and great-grandmother had to make, although I suspect she might, but that in years to come she might understand more about what these have been.

As a mother, I know that I have many faults, and I realize with sometimes uncomfortable clarity just how powerful my role is, the possibilities for a mother to be both angel and witch. Having come full circle from the days of angst and trying too hard, of resenting the narrow confines and difficulties of my own upbringing, I can now see what Mum and Nana gave me. I have worked hard, in a number of ways, to accept this legacy and to move on to create a new one for my own family. I have been able to see that my son's assessment of me is actually entirely fair, if you'll excuse the pun, and that I'm happy, now, to be a 'fairly' good mother.

*

Minutes of ICA meeting, Windgap Guild, 1966:

Talks:

Cane Work and basketry; Irish crochet;
Do Irish Mothers Spoil their Sons?; If you
had a Day to Spend as you Wish; Tweed
Pictures; Symposium on Modern Poultry
Management.

Competitions:

Tonguetwisters; pincushion; best apple tart,
St Brigid's Cross; the most attractive parcel.

Social half-hour:

How Many things to Fit in a Matchbox; Dear
Sir or Madam; Party Games of all Kinds.

Take It from Me

* We all want to make our children's lives comfortable nowadays, to spare them the repression of our seen-and-not-heard childhoods, to save them from any burdens or upset, but this isn't exactly adequate preparation for the world, where they may not get what they want, when they want it. Boy, will they get a shock when the smooth progress of their lives is interrupted, as it eventually will be, and they don't have the skills to cope with it. I am chief among the comfort-givers and am uncomfortably aware, sometimes, of just how lovely my children's lives are and, whilst I don't want to send them off to boot camp in Afghanistan to shake them up a bit, I realize that a little bit of adversity does no harm. To cycle to school in a drizzle will not actually kill them, nor will having to confess to the teacher that they, not I, forgot their maths homework.

* I try to teach my children a reasonable amount of discipline: to do their homework, to turn up to school and after-school activities, to work reasonably hard. I know that I'm a bit of a softie, forgetting to get them to practise their karate and reading and only occasionally remembering my daughter's music, but good behaviour and manners I insist on, to a dragon-like level. And whilst I frequently demonstrate the opposite characteristic, I hope that some of my efforts will pay off.

* It can be tempting as a mother to be harder on one's daughters, to withhold the praise and encouragement

that we offer our sons. It's an ancient Irish tradition not to let our daughters get too many high-flown ideas, to find their successes and achievements so much harder to stomach, when we tell our sons that they are God's Gift. This creates two problems: men who think they are Napoleon when they are pretty bog-standard and women with no self-confidence and low self-esteem. Appropriate praise is invaluable, as is, I think, some extra encouragement for our daughters: after all, we women know something of what lies ahead.

* I frequently blow a gasket with my children, losing my temper in an unseemly manner, barking at them or banging the door loudly behind me as I exit the room (who's the child, I sometimes wonder?). Occasionally I feel I literally cannot stand another fight or come across another mess and I fume and rage accordingly, or sometimes I just pick a fight because I am under pressure and it's easy to take my anger out on the kids. Then I chide myself that I'm a bad mother, a monster, and whilst I know I'm probably not, I need to do some deeper thinking about why I react the way I do and if I can change this before all my kids remember of me is Mrs Angry – I sense it will be a lifelong struggle, but we all have our weaknesses as mothers and, thankfully, our strengths.

Chapter Eight

Frenemies: the Mothering Community

'After tea, a social half-hour consists of short plays or dramatic games or mimes acted by members.

Sometimes there is dancing or community singing. One of the members, a grandmother, undertook at short notice to take the part of the Ghost in a burlesque of "Hamlet", another sustained alone an impersonation of Nero, complete with toga and laurel wreath.'

Irish Countrywomens Association claim to a bequest from the late Charlotte Shaw, January 1952

As this enthusiastic description of an ICA meeting from the 1930s demonstrates, there is something of the girl scout about the notion of a 'group' of mothers, all knitting away, chatting pleasantly, sharing tips and swapping recipes, something wholesome and home baked. The picture is one of happy women enjoying an evening away from their children and indulging in a little am-dram, as well as sharing gossip and supporting each other in a high-spirited, faintly girlish manner.

A description of any group of women will inevitably include words like sharing, support, warmth and companionship. After all, there is no one else who can relate to the joys and rages, the frustrations and disappointments of being a mother better than another mother, who can nod her head as you recount the latest story of Johnny's temper tantrums and Jane's teething, and proffer her own examples which will make you feel immediately reassured and sometimes a tiny bit smug at the idea that your children are so much better behaved. Other mothers will share the experience of being a mother, the knowledge of what changes you as a woman when you become a mother: the bits that sag, the other bits that don't work any more, the unsympathetic husbands, or the supportive ones, the greying hair, piles and mild incontinence, the loss of status and economic power. Other mothers will snort with laughter along with you as you recount some maternal indignity or murmur in sympathy as you confess the fact that some days you would rather shoot yourself than put up with the kids' screaming.

When I was growing up, busy ladies were part of the landscape, my mother and her friends constantly beavering away, a hive of jam-making, recipe-sharing, knitting, dog-walking. There was a crisp efficiency to their dealings, a no-nonsense vibe which befitted their status as busy homemakers, but there was also a more casual sharing to their lives, a quiet solidarity which nowadays is harder to find, because we no longer have the time or the need for the social groups that were so essential to my mother and grandmother: we have 'real' jobs and earn 'real' money and the parents' committee is for the women who have time, i.e. nothing better to do. The charity committee is strictly for the ladies who lunch and even the mother and toddler group, which got me through my children's babyhood, is now largely attended by carers for the purpose of comparing salaries and bitching about their bosses. But although we may not band together in lovely, helpful groups, all knitting for Ireland, or making jam, sharing recipes and practising Irish dancing, as did the

ICA, valiantly supporting rural women as they kept their families afloat in the grim early years of the twentieth century, we still need other mothers to support us in our daily slog.

Modern motherhood comes with built-in isolation that requires real effort to dislodge. At the baby clinic or park, you strike up conversations with other mothers, cooing at their little bundles and swapping war stories. You bond casually over the swings whilst keeping an eye out for your wayward toddlers, swapping stories of teething and bed wetting, good pre-schools and handy tips for entertaining them on wet afternoons. You tend to make friends with complete strangers because of your babies, and only realize after a while that they hold ultra-right wing views, or are members of the Taliban, or the Christian Mother's Alliance for the Propagation of the Faith. This doesn't matter much, because your willingness to make connections, to reach out to other mothers, overcomes social quibbles, but also because most of these casual encounters end at the park gates and then you go home, by yourself, and watch *Ready, Steady, Cook* and play with your children or make the dinner, in your own little bubble until the following day when you connect with another mother over the supermarket aisle or in the swimming-pool changing room. And sometimes you don't – you have gone back to work after maternity leave, or, like me, work from home and so can't tune into the circuit when you feel like it. That as a mother you are basically alone with your children has been one of the unexpected realities of my mothering experience and has coloured my thinking about this real or imagined 'community'.

And there is also a less-talked-about Dark Side to mothering, a harshness in our judgements of other mothers that reflects the unwelcome harshness that we women can display to each other in other areas of our lives: whether it be the secret assessment of another's shortcomings as a mother, the affirmation that you would never let little Sebastian go to bed at ten/suck a dummy/ eat jellies, or the 'advice' which is, in fact, unhelpful criticism, delivered with a smile but guaranteed to fill the unfortunate recipient with anxiety about her own mothering abilities.

So, how do we find support nowadays, from our friends or family, in the book group, the bake sale, casual exchanges in the office canteen about Mary's progress at gym class and Johnny's exam results? Has the way that we offer support to mothers really changed that much from the Victoria-sponge-and-cups-of-tea of Nana's time? Is the reality now a judgemental bitchfest or something more profound and even hopeful?

*

Both Nana and Mum would have been surrounded by familial bedlam when they returned home from hospital with their babies. Arklow wasn't far enough away for Nana to escape her large family, who would all have taken the bus down from Dublin to see the new arrival, expecting a cup of tea and a slice of apple tart after the 30-mile journey, if not a nice home-cooked dinner. And when my mother returned home from hospital with her first baby to a houseful of relatives, I can't help thinking she would have welcomed a bit of crushing loneliness. But the idea was only then taking hold that a husband and wife might live in their own home – alone. Until that time, it was considered entirely normal for a young couple to move in with the in-laws, as did my mother with Dad's colourful granddad: loneliness was not the problem, but rather privacy and space to develop as a mother without Granny hanging over you at every opportunity telling you that you were doing it all wrong.

Now, in our nuclear, suburban world, we have all the privacy we need and to make contact with other human beings, particularly when you have a tiny baby, can require Herculean effort. You can often stay marooned in the house for a day, unable to summon up the energy or the will to dress yourself or the baby, to change his/her nappy, change him again because he has thrown up on his babygro, or done a mustard poo all the way down his legs, or he wants to feed just as you are going out the door. Eventually, you give up and stare glumly at *Dr. Phil* for the afternoon.

I survived the early days of my son's life thanks to the support of my lovely community midwives, a bunch of cheerful, practical women who called in every single day for the first month to dispense advice and to chat for half an hour, providing me with just the kind of support I needed. And, when I would settle myself down on the sofa in front of *Bargain Hunt* of a morning, feeding my son, a polite phone call would invite me to one of my antenatal friends' homes for lunch, or to the park, where we would sit under the dripping trees, it being the wettest summer in many years, and drink tea and eat sausage sandwiches and discuss in puzzlement what was happening to us, how many stitches we'd had, how difficult breast-feeding was, whether we'd ever sleep again, what those peculiar noises little Jim made might be. Trips were organized to Ridley Road market to purchase four mangos for a pound, or to the posh baby shop in Stoke Newington, or to the zenith of our maternal excitement, John Lewis baby department, a Mecca of buggies, toys, clothes and all kinds of baby paraphernalia whose use was unclear. We discussed the merits of electric breast pumps, washable nappies, buggies, nap times, cot mobiles and marvelled at the number of chocolate biscuits we were consuming. We also talked about ourselves, and the changes in our lives and our sense of self, how there was no time to blow our noses, let alone shower, and how we would wait all day for our partners to return in order to get a decent meal, and about how lost we felt sometimes, how we doubted that we would ever have a 'normal' life again – we wouldn't, but it was perhaps best not to know. We were all charting these waters of first motherhood together and when I veered wildly off course they were there to offer sympathy and lifesaving support.

There is nothing like having babies to pull you towards other young mothers, regardless of your social differences. Childbirth is a great leveller. Mary may be pulling down 200K in the City and you might be a part-time pottery teacher, but you both had to push your babies out into the world in the same undignified manner, urged on by a midwife, in the same hospital. You both face the same anxieties about sleeping, feeding, winding, weight-gain, and about your own body. When you have a baby, it's the one time in your life when you can drop the social niceties and make connections with other mothers, free of the silent assessments we all make about each other, which help us decide whether this person is 'one of us' or not. Other mothers know what you've been through and how gorgeous and remarkable your baby is. However, as our children grow and we move on from the early days of handwringing ineptitude, our social antennae emerge once more, as we make subconscious and sometimes not so subconscious lists of our differences as mothers. When we move on to the larger social groupings outside the home, it can be a bit of a jungle out there.

*

Parent-and-toddler groups didn't exist when my mother was a young mother. There was no need: all of your peers were at home just like you and you would bump into countless people on your way to the shops, making way on the pavement for each other's huge prams. In my mother's small corner of suburban Dublin each house contained a mother and several children, and so the route from home to shop or post office would take her into lots of small social encounters with other mothers. My mother formed great friendships in this way that endure to this day, in spite of my brother's efforts to kill their children. One of my mother's earliest friends was Vivienne, who had moved in up the road to her husband's family home, which came complete with father-in-law. Meetings would never be arranged but either Mum or Vivienne would appear on each other's doorstep with some vague pretext and be invited in for a cup of tea, or a peruse of the *Freezer Cookbook*, whilst we children would be hustled 'outside to play' in a force-ten gale. Dogs would be walked and tantalizing snippets of gossip would be exchanged and some food item would change hands. When my mother went into hospital to have my baby sister, I stayed with Vivienne and couldn't wait to leave because her food wasn't nearly as nice as Mum's. They didn't need the kind of formal social groupings that we have nowadays, with casual encounters on the pavement less frequent. These days, new mothers and occasionally fathers stave off the loneliness of the toddler years by joining the parent-and-toddler group, a collective that is both awful and great at the same time, a microcosm of mothering society and a minefield of social faux-pas, replete with interesting sociological observations.

There is a time and a place for the mother and toddler group. With small children to entertain and the day stretching ahead uncertainly, its benign pleasures can be a godsend – the jigsaw table, the cutting and sticking board, the scuffles that break out over the toy car – an oasis of sociability in an otherwise lonely day. The opportunity to have contact of any sort with others over two is welcome and you'll even put up with having to sing 'Bob the Builder' fifty times at song time in order to do so: you are happy that your child is happy and has a whole new room of toys to wreck and children to hit and that you have an hour's liberation from *Peppa Pig* DVDs and lonely Lego building. And yet when the social circle widens, you can hardly imagine how you ever sat in an overheated room, drinking lukewarm tea, listening to another mother banging on about how she never fed her child processed food and when was a good time to enrol them for Suzuki violin.

At this stage, it is the differences rather than the similarities in your mothering that become apparent. Unlike your antenatal friends, you haven't seen each other in a greying maternity bra and saggy underpants, or wrestling with a baby's nappy on a wobbly public-toilet changing table; that close bond of solidarity forged in mutual vulnerability isn't there. At parent and toddler, you will see other mothers feeding theirs a bourbon cream and reflect that you would never let little St John eat anything other than Fair Trade Madagascan rusk; or you might have no problem with Ribena and fish fingers, but other mothers throw their hands up in horror unless absolutely everything isn't organic. One mother pounced on me in the group one day because my son had offered hers his beaker of apple juice, which her child had gratefully accepted and begun to swig from like a thirsty pirate. She shrieked, 'But Bua' – the fashion in Ireland is to call your child after some remote Celtic warrior these days – 'Bua doesn't drink anything but *filtered water*!'

But such skirmishes are rare, as the veneer of niceness which comes to dominate our encounters as mothers comes to the fore. The code of conduct of the parent-and-toddler group, and indeed of all social groupings from now on, is that polite conversation *only* is allowed. No talk about second homes on Cape Verde, no moaning about the recession and absolutely no politics. One mother of my acquaintance used to break this rule with impunity, banging on about how pernicious she thought George Bush was – hardly a novel observation, and one that probably didn't need airing at ten o'clock on a wet Thursday when we all just wanted a bit of peace and a bit of mild chat about where we were going on our summer holidays. The sort of conversation that you might enjoy in another setting becomes dynamite in the polite confines of the mother-and-toddler group.

Which is why you might find kindred spirits in mother-and-toddler, but not necessarily. I hung around on the fringes of a few groups, but couldn't seem to find a niche for myself within them. Unlike in the antenatal group, where I felt entirely comfortable admitting that I felt lost sometimes, I couldn't help feeling that I had to present an idealized version of myself as a mother in playgroup – one who was selfless, patient, endlessly nurturing, solicitous of my child's welfare, not the demented, frazzled mother who gave her child fish fingers because she didn't have the energy to do anything else, or reprimanded him a little too enthusiastically when he misbehaved. If you were anything other than exemplary, or dared present another, less acceptable facet to yourself, you would find yourself the recipient of the silent but lethal assessment of other mothers. And this Nice/Nasty dichotomy, with the silent judgements, the comparisons and the sizings-up buried beneath a sheen of ninja-warrior niceness, continues on into school and life.

*

The ICA provided Nana with an outlet for her interest in country pursuits and with an instant group of friends, but also with a job; the Association was an interest group, and as such, various committees were set up to look into rural development, into cabbage propagation, into the extortionate cost of funerals, or providing violin lessons to women in country towns – Nana was permanently busy on a range of sub-committees and in the skills training centre, the splendidly named Termonfeckin, where she would give courses in rug-making, flower-arranging and skin-curing. In my mother's case, the parents' association at my sister's primary school was her outlet and her group of women co-organizers made for a formidable lot, bustling around with clipboards and tabling motions to the Minister for Education. The fact that one member found her way into politics through the parents' committee and would later become a government minister proved that groupings such as these were a legitimate outlet for women's ambitions which were thwarted elsewhere. Now, my ambitions are fulfilled in my work, so I don't have any need for the nice ladies on the school committee, do I?

I arrive in the schoolyard at 2.30 p.m. every day and have pleasant chats about educational challenges, who's bullying who, whose got headlice and who hasn't. I have lovely friends among the other mothers and if ever I need my children collected, or minded for a bit, or can't get to school on time, another mother will step in, just as I will when asked. We share lifts to parties and swimming-pool rotas and quietly share stories about our children's bad dental habits, the best secondary schools, the latest football classes. School is a mine of useful information and a great support network. It is also a kind of rite of passage, the transition from the narrow confines of buggy, shopping centre and park to the broader horizons of Gaelic football practice, rugby, scouts. Suddenly the world opens up and becomes full of bustling activity. From the day stretching ahead into infinity, now the days pass in a busy whirl of dropping, fetching, homework supervising, dentists' visits, singing lessons, etc.

But the school community, too, has its careful social rituals, its codified behaviours, and getting to grips with it all can feel like learning another language, one which, I'm ashamed to say, I don't speak with any fluency. Perhaps I think that I have other things to be doing? After all, it's not like it was fifty years ago, is it? Last year, it was my daughter's class's turn to help out at the Communion Breakfast – a party held in the school hall after First Holy Communion for parents and children. We are not religious but I felt sure I'd be able to manage making a few sandwiches and pots of tea without God striking me down. And so I arrived with my Tupperware containers of ham sandwiches, which I'd been asked to make. Of course, I hadn't taken the crusts off because I'm a complete pleb and I looked at Audrey's perfectly manicured set with envy – making a mournful mental note of another thing I'd got wrong. We put out trays of food on the tables under Mary's tutelage, arranging things precisely at the angle she designed. She was quite particular and I had to fight the urge to place the trays at a peculiar angle just to subvert the whole process – I think I have a problem with authority. And then a polite discussion broke out about how to keep the tea urns constantly heating when they took about an hour to come to the boil and half of Dublin was due any minute for tea and sandwiches. Panic set in and polite exchanges about adding warm water from the taps or filling the urns with boiling water from the kettle became increasingly acid as one woman fought the urge to beat another over the head with the large metal object.

It was amusing to watch, for a while, marvelling at how a pecking order quickly established itself, with bossy Hilda taking control with her seating plan and telling us all what to do, clashing with equally bossy Mary as she laid out the cups and saucers in the shape of a cross, Audrey and Joan running around after her asking her what they should do next and the rest of us trying to pretend we were doing something useful whilst just running back and forth in an aimless fashion. I began to long for my bed. It was now lunchtime and I hadn't eaten since eight that morning, but I was determined not to tuck into the platefuls of unhealthy snack food before me because I was on one of my periodic attempts to lose weight, which involved stupidly eating one slice of toast for breakfast then starving for the next few hours, before giving up and wolfing down four Creme Eggs. I ferried food in and out to the tables and made sure Granny had a nice cup of tea and Aunty Anne a decent selection of — crustless — sandwiches, mine having been carefully left behind in the kitchen. Eventually, I returned to the kitchen balancing a stack of saucers in my hands and promptly passed out. I came to with a circle of other mothers surrounding me, offering me sugary drinks and murmuring about whether I might be having a heart attack. 'You need to get your blood pressure checked,' one of them, a nurse, remonstrated. I smiled and nodded and accepted 7UP and sweet tea, absolutely mortified at my unseemly display and also, if I'm honest, at the genuine kindness of these women, some of whom, until five minutes previously, would have given Stalin a run for his money. Over the following few days, a flurry of texts and calls enquired about my health and made suggestions for doctors to see/treatments to pursue. And whilst a friend of mine joked that I was probably allergic to the Communion Breakfast, it was a real learning for snobby old me. Part of me thought all of this sandwich-making was beneath me, that community was for wimps, but was reminded, to my shame, that this is not the case.

*

There's no denying, though, that there's a rigidity in our social encounters nowadays, which are carefully codified, organized and regimented, both our social lives and our children's are organized with huge amounts of advance planning, carefully fitted into the crammed extra-curricular calendar, the frantic school-homework-dancing/tennis/football cycle that sucks us in and spits us out much, much later, wrung-out shadows of our former selves.

As a child, every so often I would announce to my mother that I wanted to invite a friend home from school and she would roll her eyes to heaven – didn't I have at least twenty friends on the road to play with? Couldn't I just walk out the door and go and play on the street with the hordes all playing tennis, or British Bulldog 1-2-3, or hopscotch? Playdates, when I was a child, were a once-yearly special treat, to be celebrated with ice-cream and lemonade and proper good manners towards your 'guest' for the afternoon. Now, playdates, even the name of which makes me clench my teeth in distress, have become the norm by which our children make relationships with others, in a carefully controlled environment, organized by polite arrangement between Mum and another mum, whom I sometimes don't even know by name. Polite texts fly back and forth until a suitable date is arrived at, fitted carefully in between pony riding and karate, four Fridays hence. I have to drive to school instead of cycling, lest Little Pollyanna think I operate some kind of boot camp and make all guests walk the mile-and-a-half home. When she arrives she won't talk or eat for a couple of hours because she's transfixed with shyness and both she and my child lurk around me, asking me what they're going to do now. Inevitably, I find myself offering to help them make buns or to pull out the ancient paddling pool and fill it if it's a sunny day, or dragging out the paints set for them to use – whatever they do, it involves my effort, whilst I try to answer several phone calls, vacuum the living room and put on another wash. And all the time I have to be nice, which I find wearing, making an effort not to raise my voice or reprimand too briskly, lest Pollyanna return home and tell her mother that her friend's mum is some kind of monster. Sometimes the strain is too much for me and I find myself emitting a shriek as paint is smeared all over the sofa and Pollyanna looks at me in barely concealed horror. And so I revert to forced jollity until the little mite is picked up by her mum and ferried home in her car.

I hate playdates with every fibre of my being, but there's no point going on about the good old days and how it used to be, when we all just played on the street, etc. Those days are gone, for a number of reasons, and getting all misty-eyed won't bring them back, nor, now that I come to think of it, all the bad stuff we also endured, like corporal punishment and abuse by those in authority in holy Catholic Ireland. What's significant about playdates is their careful arrangement and planning, which makes me slightly nervous for my children's social skills: will they be able to make social judgements about others when they get older if they haven't made their own friendship choices, will they be able to be active participants in their own communities if they haven't had any experience in being pro-active as children? And sometimes, the subtle undercurrent of social selection that takes place, with the 'right' children being invited and not Mary with her challenging behaviour and grubby clothes, can be heartbreaking. Occasionally, I have the uneasy feeling that there is something Darwinian at work in the seemingly innocuous playdate, which reflects our anxiety as mothers about the world in general. It's a jungle out there, and if your child is not attending the Academy for Gifted Children or doing extra maths, if after school you simply come home and, well, hang around instead of ushering your child to another carefully selected activity, you might as well admit to neglect. If as a mother or father, you don't go along with the scheduling and the development-focused parenting, you can find yourself outside the group, marginalized by the sheer fact that you are not meeting Monica three times a week in the swimming pool, or aren't on the rota for cross-country running or lacrosse or soccer. Your child is not in the elite and neither, by extension, are you.

*

Of course, there is no reason, I suppose, why women should form a sort of collective group hug, to display the supportive warmth and emotional connection which, we are told, is absent in communities of men, which keeps us here in the home where we should be and men butting heads in the boardroom. Perhaps it is simple sexism to suggest that women should display these essentially 'feminine' traits of caring, empathy and a sense of the collegiate and yet I think it's essential that we should and that we do: the world has plenty of ass-kicking and flying testosterone as it is. It's a pity that the school or playgroup is considered the only acceptable place to display these skills rather than in the killing fields of the office, but there we go.

In modern communities, more fragmented and diffuse than in Nana's and Mum's day, we mothers are terribly nice to each other. We smile and wave, and listen politely and offer advice, but we also silently judge and criticize, particularly in the schism between mothers who work and those who don't. Mothers who stay at home, who, it is implied, have made sacrifices to spend time with their children, can make harsh judgements about those who have chosen not to. That these women are somehow less concerned about their children's welfare, less solicitous of their optimum development and well-being, is an opinion I have heard from the lips of some at-home mothers, and which I have found mildly alarming. That they are not present at the school fundraisers or unable to oblige with the school rota, that their children turn up to the cake sale with – gasp! – shop-bought cake makes them somehow unworthy of the role of mother, which only a woman who devotes her entire being to her children can assume. In the same way, working mothers see at-home mums as filling in the endless time at their disposal with a range of 'little woman' activities like tennis and coffee mornings, the gym and walking the dog. At-home mothers have nothing else to do, after all, and devote themselves to their children because they hadn't the ambition to cut it in the office and so they potter aimlessly around the school, trying to pester the teachers and volunteering for anything going.

We all know that this isn't true – that the choices we mothers make are more complex than a simple one between selflessness and selfishness, between ourselves and our children, and yet we don't help matters by having a go at 'the other side' when the opportunity arises. Constantly slinging arrows across the divide, we forget to acknowledge our common goals and concerns as mothers. We all want our children to be happy, independent, healthy. Some of us feel that we can't survive as women without some degree of personal fulfilment, others find peace and job satisfaction in the home, and whatever choices we make are the right ones for us, but not necessarily for others. Devoting ourselves entirely to our children doesn't inevitably mean that they will turn out to be prodigies just because they have been the focus of all our ambition and attention and, yes, if we work, we acknowledge that we make sacrifices in time and our availability to our children – we are not always there with a tray of scones or a packed swimming bag, and this isn't a bad thing, it just is.

And we well-educated mothers, with a wealth of information at our fingertips, a life of relative privilege compared to many others and indeed to our own mothers, fuss dreadfully, getting into a state if our child shares a beaker with another, or bashes them over the head with a Thomas the Tank Engine train or gets on a slide without holding Mummy firmly by the hand in case they might fall and bump their head and endure a subdural haematoma and need permanent hospitalization. The world we live in, this logic says, is fraught with danger, a minefield of accidents waiting to happen, and it is our duty to prevent risk of any kind. It seems that motherhood has become an evolutionary minefield for many of us and rather than support each other through it, or ask ourselves searching questions about whether we are right to see the world in this way, we silently assess each other's shortcomings and find each other wanting, too afraid to be the one to say that we've got it all out of proportion, to be the parent somehow less concerned for their child's welfare. It's great to be nice – we all need it – but there is also room for greater honesty about motherhood and a sharing of real opinions, not the ones we think won't offend others.

For me, the notion of 'community' means a lot of things. It doesn't mean hand-knitted egg cosies or home-baked cakes, a poem about the visit of the Pope, a floral arrangement made out of corrugated cardboard; it doesn't even mean a bit of horizon-broadening travel, or a girls-together outing, the sharing of a common experience when nothing else was available. What it does mean is the ability to connect with others in ways in which, yes, women excel; to make the effort to cast aside the loneliness and isolation that are a feature of our world, to share in other's experiences of motherhood and to gain reassurance and support; sure, to share a bitch about Paris Hilton or Jordan's new nose, or how flash the Murphys have become with their new chav wagon, but to refrain from criticizing Jane's 'neglect' of little Crispin and her failure to take herself in hand after Katie's birth and banish that cellulite. To acknowledge our inner mean spirit, the sprite that urges us to make nasty judgements about Audrey's parenting skills and to embrace real, rather than fake niceness. To be kinder, as well as 'nicer', mothers.

*

'Please send a full report to Kerry of any activities your Guild has undertaken which might come under the title of Good Works, such as Parties, or Outings for Old People and Children, Hospital Visiting, Dances, Whist Drives, Concerts for a Charitable Object, Work for the Blind or other disabled people; Blood Transfusion. Last Tuesday, the Wireless for the Blind sale was held in the Mansion House and the ICA stall was well supported by Guilds from all over the country. It was manned by members of Dublin TA and raised £15'

Minutes of the ICA Regional Committees, Ennis, 1958

Take It from Me

* Small kindnesses are what matters to us as mothers, rather than grand gestures; the offer of a playdate, or to take your friends' kids to the park are more useful than a bunch of flowers or the vague suggestion that 'we must have lunch some time'. Lunch is the last thing a busy mother needs when she has a house full of children, mess and a work deadline looming. Practical support is the key for busy mothers, who will reciprocate when you are under pressure.

* I try not to get too excited about other mothers' ways of doing things, which I inevitably compare to mine and, of course, find mine wanting. Other mothers always seem so beatific, so pleasant compared to me, who acts first and thinks later. That is, until I remind myself that my children only have me, not lovely Olive with her homemade biscuits and endless patience, and that comparing myself with others will not benefit my children in any way. However, talking to other mothers about what works for them with their children does – I have been greatly reassured to hear that others are struggling with a grumpy tweenager or a stroppy five-year-old and have found their advice and support really useful.

* Which brings me to the thorny subject of advice – try only to give it to other mothers when asked. 'I always think . . .' or 'Have you tried . . .' are distinctly unwelcome to a mother who is trying to soothe a crying child, or at the end of her rope with their sulky, smelly teenager who hasn't washed or spoken

in three weeks. Try to listen and only proffer advice if it is requested, when you will then look like the wise old sage that you are, rather than an interfering old bat.

* Some of us are 'groupies' and some of us aren't. I love having chats and making friends, but I would sooner sit on hot coals than join a fundraising committee; I am not entirely sure that I would have made much of an ICA member, as I would have been unlikely to join in the country dancing or the sing-songs, but that doesn't mean that I am a friendless pariah, or that I can't make a contribution in other ways. There are lots of ways to help other mothers and organizing cake sales is only one of them. And yes, I do feel guilty that I can't always join in the organized jollity because I have a deadline looming, but I try my best.

Chapter Nine

How Mothers Are Seen and How They See Themselves

'In particular, the State recognises that by her life within the home, woman gives to the State a support without which the common good cannot be achieved. The State shall, therefore, endeavour to ensure that mothers shall not be obliged by economic necessity to engage in labour to the neglect of their duties within the home.'

Irish Constitution, 1937, Article 41.2

Motherhood was an important job in 1937 and when Nana became a mother, in September of that year, the then-Taoiseach, Eamon de Valera, was putting the finishing touches to his vision of the country, which was just beginning its independence. This included the rather quaint view of motherhood quoted here, which used to make us snort with derision during history lessons: to us liberated young women with the world at our fingertips, Dev's vow to make it possible for mothers to stay in the home to perform their vital duties and not to have to bother themselves with nasty work, to keep Irish mothers chained to the kitchen sink, knitting, doing Irish dancing and making enough apple tarts to last a lifetime, seemed hilariously far-fetched. But the fact is motherhood then was a job with real status. As a mother, Nana was a beacon of respectability, the centre of the family and the fulcrum of the community, and the Irish powers-that-were were simply recognizing this fact. If there was a stereotype in Nana's day, it was that of the unimpeachably respectable middle-class woman, above reproach in any way, who shopped carefully, dressed nicely and behaved as respectable middle-class women should: who tended a nice herbaceous border and made scones for the craft fair. An appearance at weekly Mass was the pinnacle of this woman's life, the chance to display her respectability to the community at large.

And whilst this clause remains in our constitution to this day, in the intervening seventy years, the status of Mother has changed, some might say diminished, to the point that it is considered by many as something that women do if they haven't managed to do something else, or are too poor to hire someone else to look after their children. Ironically, at the same time, we have been subjected to the increasing Martha Stewart-ization of the role of übermom, consulting *How to Have the Perfect Birthday Party* books for that *High School Musical*-themed party and being told that nothing less than perfection will do on the domestic front. And, whilst we may not wear roll-ons any more, we are under greater pressure than ever to look foxy, aged forty, as if motherhood hasn't had even the slightest effect on us – we are as slim, polished and gorgeous as we were when we were twenty-five. The stereotypes of Nana's day have been replaced by new ones, which decree that mothers are either sexless or foxy, bossy madams or tight-assed control freaks, devoted mother or gin-slugging lush. Where did it all go wrong?

*

A few months ago, I received a visit from one of the stream of people that call to my door, trying to persuade me to become a Jehovah's Witness or selling me Sky+ boxes before they realize that I am one of that tribe of nonentities, the Buggy Pushers. This young man was a fundraiser from an animal shelter and he stood at the door in his car coat, pin-striped trousers and beanie hat, a disconcerting mixture of street and respectable. Unable to discern my status at the doorstep, he solemnly brandished a picture of a tatty horse in my face – a miserable-looking specimen with a raggy mane and filthy coat, a dismal, hunted look in his eyes – the horse, that is – and Beanie proceeded to rattle off statistics about animal cruelty and asked me if I realized what some people did to their animals. I nodded my head and pretended to listen, keeping an ear out for shrieks from the living room, where my youngest was 'entertaining' a playmate for the afternoon.

Alerted to the fact that there was a juicy bit of unpleasantness occurring on the doorstep, my children appeared with the friends they'd been entertaining, all five of them. Beanie's confidence changed to mild alarm as twelve eyes looked at him, but, fair dues to him, he persisted, unable to back gracefully out of the situation without actually saying, 'I see that you are a mere housewife in a frumpy fleece and with a mop in your hand and therefore incapable of taking a stand against animal cruelty,' and so he went on about percentages and statistics.

I decided to let him off the hook. 'Are you looking for

money?' I enquired, interrupting his patter, 'Because I don't have any money right now.'

'Oh, no,' he replied proudly, flashing even white teeth, 'We can't do that, we're not allowed, you see.'

'Oh, well, what exactly are you looking for?' I smiled at him, shushing my four-year-old who was loudly and repeatedly asking, 'What's wrong with that horse, Mum?' whilst his friend kept up a mantra of, 'Can I go to the toilet, Alison?'

'Well,' Beanie looked at me doubtfully, sure that this derelict specimen would be unlikely to provide it, 'a direct debit of twenty-two euro a month will save this horse from certain death,' and he half-heartedly waved Misery Horse's distressing image in front of me again. 'But I can't deal with it now,' I replied, 'because as you can see, I'm quite demented!' unable to believe, as I said them, that I was actually uttering those words. Beanie man looked at me pityingly, saw the mad, middle-aged woman with the screaming children and stained jumper, folded the photo of the tatty horse up neatly, and slunk off up the street.

To this man, I was the living embodiment of just one of the stereotypes that abound about mothers nowadays. The same women, seventy years ago, who were the centre of their communities, the rock on which the country was built, the real strength behind so many rural and city families as Ireland moved towards independence, are now either MILFS or Yummy Mummies, brain-dead botoxed blondes in designer coats, or harassed, red cheeked, snot-stained mums in practical leisurewear, pushing the buggy miserably through the supermarket, wailing children behind her.

The Frumpy Fleece is a woman who has begun to sag downwards into the territory of the comfortable bosom, the hold-you-up knicker and the practical walking shoe. Harassed, unglamorous, always batting away large numbers of children at the checkout, or unloading them from a seven-seater car, the visual display of just how unfoxy she is. Mothers like us 'forget ourselves' in the supermarket or the bakery counter and witter on about the weather and fumble for change as the Latvian shop assistant rolls her eyes to heaven. We chatter away to ourselves like demented eejits, trying to keep in our head the constant roster of activities and duties that need to be entered and crossed off our schedule; we can be found carrying armfuls of coats and bags after our children at the school gates, like the emperor's slave, walking three paces behind our royal liege; we can be seen unashamedly sniffing our small babies' rear ends for any tell-tale smells, or asking our older ones at five-minute intervals if they need the loo. Frumpy Fleece is the kind of mother we wake up one day and find, to our horror, we have become.

How unlike Kate Moss Mom, all pointy nine-inch-heeled shoe-boots, striding foxily across the schoolyard, looking eminently shaggable and utterly terrifying, to pick up her tousle-haired urchin. Kate Moss mother is emphatically not One of Us – her pelvic floor remains as springy as a trampoline, her stomach muscles taut as a drum, her bosom as pert as a sixteen-year-old's – no greying, saggy M&S underwear for her. When Nice Marjorie from the school parents' committee approaches her to tap her for a round of sandwiches for the Cat's Refuge fundraiser, Kate Moss looks at her as if she has entirely lost her marbles, the implication being that she would be far too busy doing something she shouldn't to make sandwiches. She rummages in her Balenciaga handbag and sticks a ten-euro note into Marjorie's hand, smiling at her vaguely as if she hasn't quite seen her through her mirror aviators. Kate Moss Mom is the mother we all wish we were, although she faintly appals us. She has managed to have a child and to remain entirely herself, although we have no idea how she does it.

Marjorie, of course, is the pillar of the parents' committee, a sensibly clad, practical woman with a brain for organization, which would have taken her far, but for her decision to put Tarquin and Maisie first. The parents' committee is an outlet for Marjorie's frustrated ambitions, which she can now unleash to the full. Marjorie is a serial sender of e-mails about the school compost heap, the table-tennis rota and the homework club, convinced that other mothers share her passion for the school which has become the focal point of her being since little Maisie started last year and she now 'has the time to help'. Majorie thinks that Kate is a disgrace to motherhood, but if she can tap her for twenty every now and then, she will: fundraising for the new school gym/library/green bin has become the focus of Marjorie's existence and has turned her into a human Rottweiler in the process.

And then there's the stereotype that could only be an invention of our era, the Yummy Mummy, with her car the size of a small house, children clad by her friend who discovered a niche in the market for well-designed children's clothes – what, another one? – her shiny blonde mane pulled casually back into a tousled-but-carefully-styled knot. Her uniform is a Juicy tracksuit if she's off to the gym, or white shirt under knit sweater, neat jeans – none of that boyfriend nonsense – and Converse. She's never intimidatingly sexy, but rather wholesomely so; she's been sensible enough to keep herself in trim, but she doesn't go on about it, only carefully to refuse the plateful of fattening scones at coffee mornings – 'No thanks, I'm off wheat – I find it makes all the difference' – as she smiles and pats her flat stomach, in silent reproach to others who don't have her self-discipline. She's practical and down to earth but would never dream of letting motherhood overwhelm her – she loves her children but still makes time for herself and has just the right amount of money to allow her to do this. Not for her the commuter slog or the push up the high street in the rain, grimly hanging onto the buggy; she is in command of her very own Starship Enterprise, a humming, ten-feet-off-the-ground four-wheel drive, which she steers around the narrow streets, nose barely peeking above the wheel. She pops in and out of the local shops, but is never spotted at the checkout in Lidl, fifteen children hanging off her. She is the kind of woman who put family first, and left her nice but undemanding job in international marketing after her second child was born so that she can talk the 'I know what it's like to be a working mother' talk, but wouldn't dream of returning to the office now, not after five years. 'Sure I couldn't talk to adults,' she laughs, making it clear that she would never put herself before her lovely children, with their carefully selected English names – Harry, Jack and Sally; she'll leave the ridiculous Irish monikers – the Ard Greimnes, the An Tua-Nuas – to her crusty female colleagues, with their obsession with organic compost and recyclable furniture.

The Yummy Mummy is a slap in the face to every right-thinking feminist, who fought so hard for women's status and rights, the right to return to her hard-won work after maternity leave and not find that Jeremy from sales had replaced her, on account of not being a woman and all. After all the sisters in the seventies did, this new, wealthy generation has turned around and said, 'No, thanks, I'd actually prefer to let my husband keep me and play house rather than use the brains God gave me.'

The Yummy is the visible expression of our society's new wealth and with the retrograde idea that there is merit in the wholesome sacrifice that she makes for home and family. The Yummy is the sworn enemy of the Grim

Working Mother, who can't understand why a perfectly intelligent woman would want to stay at home and drive around to various shopping centres, coffee shops and tennis clubs. Grim Working Mother races into the school-yard in the morning with her ID tags around her neck, car keys in her hand and preoccupied look on her face – she hasn't got time to talk with the ladies chatting outside the school door, or to harass Johnny's teacher for the umpteenth time because he isn't making 'enough' progress in English Made Easy; she needs to drop them quick and get through the traffic to the board meeting. Grim Working Mother will nod distractedly at the few mothers she knows and they will smile politely back, silently reflecting that they haven't seen Ursula in the school since the Christmas play four months previously. Marjorie wonders how on earth she could be keeping up with her children's progress if she isn't present in their lives as she should be, expressed in a bland but meaningful, 'Ursula's always so *busy*, isn't she? I had to take Johnny home three times last week when she didn't make it back from the conference in Geneva. Not that I minded: the poor thing's rushed off her feet since the latest au pair left.' In this one seemingly innocuous statement, Marjorie skewers the unfortunate Ursula: as a working mother she neglects her children and is a serial au-pair abuser to boot.

It's interesting that in Nana's and Mum's time, negative stereotypes were also about working mothers, who were considered vaguely terrifying, leaving their children in the care of some young girl from Donegal in order to do something that was considered unnecessary and a bit intimidating, 'Sheila *works*,' it would be whispered, as if Sheila was in fact robbing banks between 9 a.m. and 5 p.m. To be fair, though, the other stereotype was the golf mother, who, even though she had 'nothing better to do', hired another girl, a poor unfortunate with no English, to mind her six children and disappeared off to amuse and entertain herself on the back nine or to meet yet another friend for lunch after her hair appointment. 'Bad' mothers were those who left their children in the care of someone else when they had no justification for it and should have been at home along with every other right-thinking mother of their generation. And then there was the woman who quietly drank the day away, about whom my mother would be heard to whisper, 'Poor Jane, she's got the blues,' accompanied by a flick of the wrist and a mime of someone swigging from a whiskey tumbler. 'The blues' was a euphemism for the chasm of alcohol into which some women fell, bewildered and frustrated by narrow horizons, undiagnosed depression and an unsympathetic society, which ignored their needs almost entirely.

The most vitriol was devoted to those women who had read feminist tomes and had joined encounter groups to 'find themselves', to see if anything lay beyond the domestic horizon, like some mad hippy infected with newfangled American ideas. Joanna Kramer, played by an icy Meryl Streep in *Kramer vs. Kramer*, a hotly discussed movie of the time, deserved to lose custody of her son to dishevelled, heartwarming Dustin Hoffman, as she had proved herself unfit by running off to find herself, the implication being that that way lay extreme danger for mothers. 'Yourself' didn't count as a mother. Your identity was bound up in the sacrifice and service you provided to your children. If you found motherhood difficult, you kept it to yourself, or helped yourself to a medicinal glass or two of wine whilst the kids burnt toast and helped themselves to a constant supply of Club Milks in lieu of dinner.

Now, negative stereotypes attach to what women *aren't* – go-getters, achievers, capable of kicking ass in the boardroom as well as putting on another wash or a nice big dinner. Those who are too dim to make it in the workplace retire nicely to mind their children, women who stay at home have Nothing Better to Do; women who work are tight-ass control freaks who gaffer-tape their children to their bunk beds in order not to miss the vital board meeting.

Of course, none of us adheres fully, or even partly, to any one role. I can be a bit of a Yummy when I feel like it, with my careful shops in the organic market and nice highlights – I, too, have eschewed the achievements of office and boardroom for my children when my mother had no such choice; I am also a Frumpy Fleece with my sensible footwear and cycling habit, my hand-wringing liberal views and earnest parenting. And I'm a Grim Working mother, too, dashing into the dance recital in between chapters five and seven, slightly distracted as I've had to push an author meeting back by an hour and need to dash off. But stereotypes exist for a reason and whilst we might poke fun at them, they tell us something about where motherhood is at right now. In the struggle between Yummy and Grim Worker bee, we find encapsulated the struggle between work and home that has consumed us over the past thirty years and which has had all sorts of unexpected consequences – the legislation that goes some way to ensuring the equality we so want, and which is our right, has not been matched by a shift in our culture; the freedom I feel as a mother, the opportunities of which I can take advantage that Nana and Mum could only dream of, are accompanied by the exhaustion of balancing my Frumpy Fleece side with my Grim Working Mother, with Kate Moss a dim and distant memory.

Since the wholesome homemakers of de Valera's time much has changed and yet the stereotypes that attach to mothers are different, but equally negative. Perhaps motherhood simply invites negative thoughts – after all, a mother is a figure who is loved, feared and reviled in equal measure; no one equals the power of the mother, the indelible imprint she has on her children's lives, the influence she wields, the ability to wreak havoc or provide a loving, supportive environment, to be Holy Mary or the

Devil Incarnate, and perhaps the stereotyping takes the sting out of this dangerous and difficult role.

*

But, as we mothers know, how we are seen by the world at large, and even by those close to us, is not necessarily who we are inside. Behind the mask we put on to present ourselves to the world lies something quite different, often darker, more turbulent, angrier, less saintly, with unfulfilled hopes and dreams, secret passions, regrets. It seems that, as a mother, in spite of all of the stereotypes, there is really only one way to present ourselves to the world, as smiling, patient, saintly, attentive to our children's needs; but what lies beneath?

Nana paid a great deal of attention to her appearance, and her morning preparations, particularly for Sunday Mass, were a sacred and lengthy ritual, one which I used to watch with fascination as a child as she would pile on layer after layer of clothes until she presented a sleek carapace to the world.

Her thermal undergarments would be put on first, a nice warm Damart vest and pants set. Then, a pair of fearsome-looking support tights, a kind of puce in colour, would carefully be unrolled and pulled gently up her legs, to meet the snappers at the bottom of her 'roll-on', a rigid girdle that stretched from the ribcage to the top of the thighs and which would be rolled on – hence the name – like a white, stretchy suit of armour. Over the roll-on-and-stockings combo would be placed a slip, if she was wearing a dress or a jumper, and slacks if she was just doing the garden, or a slip, suit and hat if Mass was on the agenda. Next, she would attend to her hair – a point of some embarrassment for Nana – a thin, wispy mane, which eventually became so depleted she used a wig. We knew that she knew that we knew that she wore a wig, but we knew better than to comment on it in any way; she would occasionally allude to 'washing my hair' with a chuckle, and another golden blonde confection would be wheeled out as a temporary replacement. So vital to her self-image was the wig that when she died, my mother was mortified to see that Nana had somehow become separated from her wig at the undertaker's – to Nana, appearances were everything.

But when I was a child, she still had her own hair and would bend over to comb it, brushing it straight out from her head until it stood upright, a shock of grey, making her resemble an elderly Krusty the Clown. She would then roll her own hair carefully over two hairpieces, rather like shoulder pads, before folding it into a rather bouffant chignon, pinned at the back with large hairpins. After this procedure, she would carefully open her powder compact and apply powder with great care, constantly checking herself in the mirror for any imperfections. And then the lipstick would be produced: generally a strong red, which suited her dark features. She would begin by outlining her lips with it and then carefully she would fill in the inside with small, deft strokes, her mouth a round 'O' in the compact mirror. She would press her lips together several times with small smacking sounds, each time examining the effect in the mirror, before reaching for a tissue, carefully folding it in two and pressing it in between her lips with a firm motion. The imprint of her lips remained on the tissue, a red smudge which she would dispatch into the waste-paper basket. Catching me watching her in the mirror, she would smile and call me over. 'Close your eyes,' she would gently order, before dabbing the musky, sweet-smelling powder over my nose. This would be followed by two soft dabs of the red lipstick. I would open my eyes and take in my powdered, lipsticked face in the mirror next to Nana's, delighted with my sophisticated appearance. 'Anyone's fancy,' Nana would smile at me, before reaching into the wardrobe for her hat of choice. This she would affix to her bouffant 'do' with great care, nudging it carefully into place until it sat just so. Her coat would then be put on and carefully buttoned, and then her best gloves, before finally the handbag, one of her Fresian numbers, the handles of which were placed gently over her gloved wrist. After her geisha-like rituals, Nana was finally ready to face the world, a respectable, glamorous lady, who could walk confidently up the church aisle – always late – and take her place in a pew near the front, knowing that she looked as she should, a respectable, middle-class woman, a pillar of the community, a mother and grandmother to whom a gentleman or younger person would politely offer their seat.

To Nana, appearances were everything to the extent that it was hard to know exactly who she really was. She had effectively left behind the turbulence and pain of her youth, the death of her beloved father, her supporting of her large family, the loss of her children, burying them behind a veneer of fabulousness and a stream of harmless chatter. 'Onne', as she called herself on the telephone, wasn't Annie as she had been christened. In the same way, my mother hid her frustrations by being in control at all times, her calm, unflappable exterior masking the emotional turbulence and stress of her family life, her almost Protestant restraint, love of gardening and *Songs of Praise* not telling the whole story of who she was. And whilst I don't need to dress in a girdle and support tights any more to present myself to the world, I don't need to put on a posh accent to disguise my Dublin tones, or even to pretend I love my life, there is a sense in which I, too, present a 'mask' to others:[14] it goes with the territory of being a mother. And somewhere, down below, is the woman I once was.

*

I was recently asked to provide a wedding photo for the fiftieth anniversary party of the priest who married my

14. Source: *The Mask of Motherhood*, Susan Maushart, Penguin, 2004.

husband and me. This photo would be shown in a montage along with all of the other happy couples whom he had married over the years. How nice, I thought as I sloped off to the shed in the garden to dig around for our wedding album. The gold-embossed book lurked under a pile of DIY manuals and drill bits and I pulled it out and blew the dust off my youth, flicking through the pages with a sense of wonder, realizing with a jolt that the young woman in the photos was actually *me*. I looked at the tiny creature hanging onto her new husband and felt like crying my eyes out.

I found it hard to pinpoint exactly why I was so upset and embarrassed; after all, I don't miss any other aspect of my younger self: the gnawing insecurity, the anxiety, the work-fixation, all of this I have exchanged cheerfully for the richer (emotionally, that is), happier self I am now, and yet . . . the change in me is clear for all to see. As I would be attending the anniversary party, I wondered if I could simply 'forget' to send in the photos: I couldn't face the mortification of being compared to my twenty-years-younger self, to have everyone point at the fat bird at table nine and reflect on the visible evidence of just how much she'd let herself go.

But it's not just that, even though I find it hard to let go of the pert, slim-waisted slip of a thing I was then, with a firm bosom, a bottom that didn't sweep the ground and a chin that stopped roughly where it should and hadn't got a nice cushion to support it; it's all the other stuff that I've had to let go of at the same time. I have more or less accepted that my more rounded form is simply the way I am now, that I will never look like Liz Hurley or Gwynnie after she did that miracle workout for her killer legs, but the passage from Pert Girl to Cushioned Mum has been hard for me emotionally, a hidden world of lost longing and some regret that the passage of time is changing me. Never again will I be chatted up by some nice man – unless he's giving me advice on drill bits or washing-machine parts; I am now a mother and, more to the point, middle aged, and therefore officially sexless. And it's unlikely that, after twenty years, my husband will faint with desire every time I walk into the room. I am no longer the centre of his universe, but must fight for his attention along with the kids and the boss; the romance of my youth is behind me and, in part, I have contributed to this.

I used to spend quite a lot of time on my appearance in the mornings before work – my careful and manic ironing was often joked about by my husband, and I would ensure my hair was blow-dried and make-up carefully applied. Now, after eighteen years of marriage, I have become blasé. My husband recently joked about my morning attire – sagging ten-year-old pyjamas and one of his T-shirts – and I was thoroughly offended – until I took a good look at myself in the mirror and concluded that he was right: how can I complain that he no longer throws me lascivious looks over the top of the *Guardian* if I look like a sack of potatoes with bailer twine around the middle?

Perhaps I'm being too devil-may-care in assuming that the longevity of our relationship will overcome his need to find someone younger and less tired-looking. I was horrified when an acquaintance recently confessed that she keeps herself whippet-thin so that her husband won't have an affair; the idea would never even occur to me, but I suppose I only have to look around me, at the legions of older men pushing their second families around, having exchanged their sexless, frumpy, blonde-highlighted wives for a nice, thin, young second wife, evidence that whilst the older model can no longer reproduce, the men sure as hell can. I realize that at the same time as waving goodbye to Pert Girl, I have also waved goodbye to my childbearing years; that at forty-three I am no longer gloriously fecund, but dried up and wizened of ovary.

And this is all the more difficult because nowadays, it's so difficult to age gracefully as a mother, when getting older is simply not allowed. You have to look shaggable, have to wear trendy clothes even though you'd secretly rather that comfortable pair of jeans with a fleece; you have to look as if you are distinctly foxy, intelligent and down with the kids. There's no sloping off to the golf club, buying floral dresses or comfortable shoes, or indulging in a spot of gardening. We middle-aged mothers ridiculously, foolishly try to compete with our daughters in a world that pities ageing and attaches such status to perfection. And celebrity magazines that fetishize motherhood, presenting various airbrushed members of the A-list as just mums like you and me, don't help. Motherhood is held up as being a full-on Gucci-clad, personal-trainer-hiring, diet-fixated, nanny-hiring extravaganza, which is a bit of a slap in the face for us mere mortals, who must content ourselves with the charity shop, the odd trip to the gym before giving up and the occasional bit of babysitting provided by Granny. Motherhood, like everything else in our lives, becomes infested with status anxiety.

*

At the same time as bidding a regretful farewell to our younger selves, we mothers are at the stage when we have survived the crises and upsets of the early years, the shapelessness of toddlerhood, and have moved into the calmer waters of primary school, with the lovely schedules and routines. Once our children's needs are no longer immediate – they no longer need us to dress them, feed them, entertain them, make them better when they've had a fall – do we return happily to our former selves? Or do our identities, in a million small ways, slowly become eroded, subsumed under a pile of laundry and making of shepherd's pies?

I recently bought myself a nice, modern white desk upon which to compose my *magnum opus*, and placed nothing else upon it but my sleek, groovy new laptop. This work surface was to be a temple to my creativity, peaceful, clean and free from the detritus that fills the rest of my life. Within a couple of hours, a Lego Star Wars soldier had found his way onto the desk, half a broken water gun and a ceramic boot my daughter had made at a birthday party. I sighed gustily, stuck a few pens into the open top of the boot and popped the mini Darth Vader into my best Honiton dish. I worked away, surrounded by my children's stuff, before going off to answer the telephone. When I returned, two dinosaurs had found their way onto the bright white surface, a large T-Rex and a velociraptor, which, if you pressed a button on its head, emitted a rather frightening shriek.

Children have a way of letting us know that they are there and that they don't have any boundaries – this bright white surface is just perfect for colonizing with their toys, after all. I like the way in which my world so comfortably becomes theirs, and congratulate myself on how much their presence is so integrated into the fabric of my working day. So what if my daughter has removed my stapler for the umpteenth time to make a horsey comic, or that nice red lever arch file now contains my son's collection of science magazines; if no Sellotape lasts longer than five minutes before it is turned into a clone matrix, wrapped around the legs of the dining room chairs, as my youngest son throws Lego bits through it, peppered by the sound of gunfire: 'Surrender now, Luke Skywalker . . .' Our lives are interconnected in the most banal and domestic ways, and the continuity is a source of great comfort and irritation to me. I construct a happy fantasy in my head of me working away whilst the children play at my feet, which carefully ignores the regular shouting – me at them to keep the noise down/stop fighting/get their fingers out of the biscuit tin, and them at each other and then me at them again – 'I'm trying to work here!'

When I worked in an office, I extracted myself every morning from their sticky embraces, waving a cheery farewell to the breakfast dishes, the stain on the front of the jumper, the toothpaste squeezed all over the basin, sinking into the embrace of the car upholstery, savouring the peace and quiet, the murmur of the news telling me how much more my house was worth than yesterday, and then in the office, the polite conversation, the occasional e-mail joke, the mutterings over the coffee machine. Nobody screamed or roared – at least not very loudly; nobody hurled books on the floor in a rage or spat their food out all over the table at lunchtime. I would revel in the hush of the editorial department, the civilized conversation, the cheerful laughter, until going-home time, when I would get sucked once more into the vortex of my children's lives, tripping over sticklebricks on the carpet, oohing and aahing over the latest pre-school paintings, dragging another pile of laundry into the machine. In work I was a real, grown-up person, fully myself, mind clear as a bell, desk untrammelled by Lego bits. At home, I was, well, Mum, back on duty at last.

When I chose to work from home, I became someone else, fused with my children in a more intimate way than I would have thought possible. My mind is no longer my own, but filled with domestic as well as work stuff: the reminder to self to post the secondary school application form sits in the same in-tray as my tax return and my latest manuscript, the diary full of dentist's appointments and reminders to buy shoes or rabbit food as well as meetings or features for the books page. My identity has become enmeshed with my children's. Who am I? I wonder. To the electricity meter reader, I'm simply that nice lady at no. 82, the only person always at home when he calls; to the annoying door-to-door charity mugger, I'm a whey-faced housewife, surrounded by children, and therefore unlikely to part with any money for his/her cause. I'm the woman who takes in the neighbours' post, who stuffs gangs of children into her seven-seater to ferry them off to the park, who waves the neighbours a cheery goodbye in the morning as she walks the youngest to pre-school. I'm my mother's daughter, an absent-minded godmother to my sister's daughter, a reasonable if vague friend. I work at the kitchen table, pushing to one side the newly fixed Limoges cake stand that my son broke when he aimed a football at it, a bunch of bananas, a hairbrush, the remains of a bunch of dying lilies, a letter from school about a cake sale in aid of cystic fibrosis. I am all of the above, but I don't feel that I am any of them, really; I am me.

I'm aware that it's a fine line between enmeshing and subsuming, between living alongside your children and drowning under a sea of laundry, dirty dishes and their casual unawareness of just how easy you make their lives, of how many classes you ferry them to in an effort to stimulate their creativity, of how many days you spend at the park chatting idly to other mothers, your mind elsewhere, of how many playdates you agree to, trying to ignore the whinging of your child's friend and the constant bickering that goes on because little Sorcha wants to play *High School Musical* and Rachel wants *Mamma Mia*. With subsuming comes depression and a lack of personal fulfil-ment, the 'tired' mothers of my childhood, lying in bed with a headache all afternoon, deciding that five-thirty was not too early for a gin and tonic after all, or haunting the sacristy in the local church, developing a tiny bit of a crush on that nice Father O'Brien. Thanks to my mother and grandmother, to their sacrifices and hard work, I no longer need to subsume, in spite of all the muddle which enmeshing creates. I am able to say that what I want and need in my life is up for consideration, along with the wants and needs of my family, although I know that there will be constant tension between the two, that personal fulfilment is acceptable, that I can love my children beyond measure and still want to be myself.

*

Daffodil Day is an annual school fundraiser, one of the many events held to raise money for charity in my children's school, in which happy participation in charity events is encouraged. All the children get cheerfully involved, baking cakes and, in this case, dressing in yellow and selling bunches of daffodils in aid of the Cancer Society. We mums shuffle into the school hall and take our places at the tables laden with yellow flowers and uncertain-looking baked goods; my son tries to sell me five bunches of daffodils for a tenner and jokes about how he and his classmates are going to reverse the three-cakes-for-the-price-of-two offer for the junior infants and see if any of them notice. I sit there with the other ladies, eating broken biscuit cake and chatting over too-strong tea. I am one of these women, I think to myself, the mothers who are always there at the school gate, tissues at the ready, who take the bags and coats and usher their children onto bicycles. I am a frumpy, stay-at-home mum with a double chin, an extra stone in weight, in my trainers and practical rain gear for the walk to school. And that's fine, because I am who I want to be and that is the great legacy of my mother's and grandmother's time. From the uncertainties of the early days when I felt lost, lonely and angry with the world for imposing on me the responsibility for another small person, when I felt love and loss in equal measure, I feel that I have grown up, just a little bit. I can't be the twenty-three-year-old I once was, and sometimes I feel nearer the age my youngest thinks I am, having misheard me once – 'My mum's sixty-three!' – but really I think I might be somewhere in between.

*

> 'The typical feature is a monthly meeting, at which business is conducted in an orderly and democratic manner, with a Chairman who may be a farmer's wife, a Secretary, perhaps a girl living at home for whom the Guild paid the fee for her to take a short, intensive course in secretarial practice, and a Treasurer, sometimes a housewife, establishing herself as a woman of unquestioned integrity.'
>
> Irish Countrywomens Association claim to a bequest
> from the late Charlotte Shaw, January 1952

Take It from Me

* Getting older as a woman is hard, especially when it is continually drummed into us how 'distinguished' men get at this age, how attractive they still are when we are drooping and sagging and past our childbearing peak. The impulse can be to 'do something' about it; to take up Bikram yoga, to get Botox, to emerge from a little teeth-whitening and skin-pulling looking 'ten years younger!' But I have had to learn to live with the fact that I am getting old and yes, I will die sooner or later, and no amount of surgery is going to halt this process. It's been hard to lose that side of myself, but I console myself with the fact that whilst others might think I am dumpy Mum, my life is richer and more varied than ever, more replete with possibility. And that Botox will only make me look weird.

* And one of the great things about getting older these days is that you no longer hugely care what people think of you; you can say no with confidence, unafraid of others' disapproval or displeasure; you can dress like a Hell's Angel or take your children to school in a milk float; you are aware of the fact that in the great scheme of things, it all doesn't matter. That we can become an embarrassment to our children is one of the most liberating and enjoyable aspects of our lives as we get older.

* When we women get together, the impulse can be to discuss in unwelcome detail our piles and sagging pelvic floors, our wonky bladders and less-than-brilliant sex lives, but I feel that such chat should be kept to a minimum. We are not yet on the over-sixties' bus tour to Clacton and a certain amount of dignity and self-control is still needed.

* It's important to acknowledge just how depressing motherhood can be sometimes. I have always felt that

a life with children means a certain amount of low-level depression, which can change even the most cheerful woman into a religious maniac, or a woman who takes to sandblasting the house to get rid of 'germs', which we are convinced lurk in every corner. It is important to get hold of something that's yours, whether it be Death Metal or stamp collecting, a sociology degree or a job; maintaining your own identity goes a long way in the battle against the depression which can often grip us mothers.

Epilogue: A Battle to the End

When I returned to Ireland eleven years ago, Nana was very much still with us, in her little flat next door, Mass blasting away on the radio as she tottered unsteadily up and down the steps to the garden. She was very fond of my son, then only a toddler, and he liked her too, her cheerful warbling and her stash of mini Mars bars, which he quickly learned to locate in the sideboard in her living room. One of the last photos taken of Nana is in her garden, hubcap-bedecked and full of flowers; she is sitting in her green plastic garden chair, gesturing to my son, whose blond head is turned to look at whatever she's showing him: there is a smile on both their faces, as if they are both sharing some great joke. Nana's steel-grey wig is only slightly lopsided on her head, and her enjoyment of her great-grandson is clear on her face.

Nana was ninety when the picture was taken, still able to walk – aided by an umbrella with a mallard's head for a handle, as she refused to get a stick – but she would list to starboard and threaten to topple over at any moment. She had been forced to stop driving, due to the fact that she could no longer see, and after a dicey encounter with a cyclist when she'd been turning out of the driveway of the Home for the Blind after visiting a friend, which made us howl with laughter – once we'd realized he was OK, of course. But my mother, who had insisted Nana come to live with them ten years before, was finding it increasingly hard to cope. She was doing more and more of the leg-work, dropping Nana to Mass every morning and picking her up after her little chat with the nice man in the front pew, and ferrying her to Roche's Stores to buy her 'nice bit of bacon' and packets of biscuits, taking her to the doctor, the dentist and everything else. Worn down after ten years of responsibility for Nana as well as for my brother, the subject that dare not speak its name – a home – was discussed. I'm not sure how, but the decision was made to look at suitable establishments and, as the eldest daughter, and thought to be a solid sort of individual, I was asked to come with them to see a home in Bray – a full 15 miles from where they lived. Mystified, I agreed. I was used to the twists and turns of their relationship at this stage and knew that my mother needed some support in this dreadful task. I could ask questions later, I reasoned.

I knew that Nana would find this hard, to be 'put away' when she had lived all her life independently and with gusto, but of course Nana never engaged with a single dark emotion in her whole life, never even admitted that she might have one, so to see her pathetic attempt at gaiety as she was ferried off to this alien place was heartbreaking. She warbled away, lowering herself into the car, her Sunday-best hat on, a jaunty trilby which she'd bought in Austria fifty years before, complete with pheasant feather in the brim, tucking her umbrella in beside her. Her face was resolute – I will not even admit to myself that this is happening – as she grinned away and made remarks about the weather, what she saw out the window, etc. My mother was tight-lipped.

We were shown around a perfectly nice place in Bray, an extended bungalow with spacious rooms that gave on to a nice garden, by a pleasant if slightly harassed middle-aged man, who congratulated Nana on only needing an umbrella: 'Oh, me,' wittered Gracie Fields, doing a little pirouette, 'I like dancing far too much to need a stick!' My mother rolled her eyes to heaven and I tried to smile. Nana jabbered on, all the time refusing to take in her surroundings, chirruping away like a busy canary until we were expelled from the front door out into the windswept car-park, gulls screeching overhead. 'Well, that was nice,' my mother said. We winched Nana into the car again. They both sat upright in the front of the car, like a pair of watchful Jack Russell terriers. I decided to maintain a silence in my seat behind them; no comment seemed necessary about the human drama unfolding before me.

After a few minutes' silence whilst we all digested Nana's fate, my mother announced: 'Now, there's a new estate here I want to have a look at.' I had known for some time that Mum and Dad had been thinking about moving house, from their too-large five-bed with huge garden, to something more manageable, and a series of estate agents' brochures had appeared on the kitchen table, for small, manageable bungalows in nice areas of the suburbs, not far from where my parents lived. But as we approached a terribly tightly packed estate of semi-ds, I wondered what on earth had got into my mother. She had sworn for so long that she couldn't wait to break free of the responsibilities of caring for Nana, and yet here she was, wanting to move to a house 200 yards from the place she had chosen for her.

As my mother walked around this rather nondescript place called something Irish and mystical, in a location that had previously never crossed her mind, I pulled her to one side: 'Mum, I thought you wanted some space, and here you are contemplating moving closer to Nana. I don't get it!' Like every self-righteous daughter, I was indignant. The logic of it didn't seem to work, my mother was being just daft and it was my duty to dissuade her from this ridiculous course of action. And yet now I understand. My mother wanted to be far away from Nana and yet she didn't. She couldn't just give up her responsibilities to her mother, no matter how much she annoyed her, to the extent that she decided to move after her, to a place in which she had no interest in living, because she felt responsible for her to the end.

And this, to me, is the lesson I learn from mothering,

that this is precisely what it takes: devotion, loyalty, love in the midst of all the irritation and angst, the seething rage, the Freudian thoughts that my mother doesn't understand me and she always liked my sister better, or that I am a terrible mother who is inflicting all kinds of psychological damage on my children. I have come some way from the lifestyle-supplement, Caroline-Ingalls vision of motherhood that filled my head before I had children. Since becoming a mother, I have found myself, at times, more depressed, lonelier and more bored than I would have thought possible, particularly in the early years of my children's lives when there was no structure to anchor me, ground down by the relentless routine, the endless tidying up after spills, the washing of grubby handprints from the paintwork and mopping the kitchen floor of sticky footprints, the constant breaking up of fights, the endless requests – 'Muummm . . .' – and now I am more frustrated by the way every task takes about ten hours with children and how I have no time or space to myself, that everything I do is – quite naturally, I accept – monitored by my curious ten- and eight-year-olds, or that my five-year-old's obsession with death and relentless questioning on the subject is wearing me down.

But I am also more content than I would ever have expected to be. Motherhood has given me the ability to love someone other than myself, which is a mercy, it has to be said. Of my children I expect nothing, I just love them and, in spite of my explosive temper, my impatience and a quixotic way of doing things, they love me back, which fact constantly surprises me and which is one of the lovely things about motherhood. To be loved simply because you are Mum, no matter what kind of a mum, is remarkable, I feel, and I have come to appreciate and even enjoy my centrality to their young lives instead of chafing against it. I have gone from being Woody Allen to the Dalai Lama, enjoying what I feel life is about – love, family, work, fun – when I can distract myself from everything I think it should be about, that is, such as a bigger house with a nice garden and an expensive kitchen and a four-wheel drive and a little man to do the garden. For all this, I thank my children. And I thank Mum and Nana for showing me how it's done. When my time comes, whether or not they shove me in a rest home with my umbrella and collection of Easy Classics CDs, I hope that my children will show me the same devotion and care as my mother showed hers.

Acknowledgements

First, because he has endured only slightly less pain than I have as this project has slowly taken shape, to Colm, for his calm forbearance, endless support, literary chats and years of putting up with my temper tantrums. Tight lines, as they say. To my mum for putting up with searching questions and for her thoughtful responses. To the sisterhood of Dublin, Shirley 'Have you done your proposal yet?' O'Rourke, Mary 'You'll be Fabulous one day' Bruton, my sister Caitriona for a lifetime's hysterical laughter; to Eleanor Kennedy and Nerea Lerchundi for coffee and irresistible gossip, and for exchanging children willingly. To the O'Gaora clan, particularly to Annette, for their interest and support. To Jill Casey and Colette Clail, sincere thanks.

On a professional level I would like to thank Marianne Gunn-O'Connor for her belief and the great care which she has shown her wayward client; to the lovely and ever-patient Pat Lynch; to my editor Georgina Morley for her enthusiasm and for hanging on in there as I sent her pathetic 'nearly-there' e-mails; for Imogen Taylor, fellow editor, for her endless kindness and news about her boys which has kept me so entertained. To the super-efficient Tania Adams and Catherine Richards at Pan Macmillan and to the irrepressible Davey Adamson. To Susan Opie and the marvellous Andrew, for a weekend's wine-snarfing and for memories of lowly editorial misery which keep me warm when I want to give up.

And of course, to my children, Eoin, Niamh and Cian, without whom, quite naturally, there would have been no book.